CHILDREN (NI) ORDER 1995

Regulations and Guidance

Volume 1

Court Orders
and
Other Legal Issues

Belfast: The Stationery Office

© Crown copyright 1996. Published for the Department of Health and Social Services under licence from the Controller of Her Majesty's Stationery Office.

Applications for reproduction should be made in writing to
The Copyright Unit, Her Majesty's Stationery Office, St Clements House, 2-16 Colegate, Norwich NR3 1BQ.

Published and Printed in the UK by The Stationery Office Limited

Dd 308036 10/96 5500

CHILDREN ORDER

The Children Order series of regulations and guidance consists of the following:

CHILDREN ORDER

PREFACE

This series of volumes of regulations and guidance builds upon "An Introduction to the Children (NI) Order 1995" published by the Department of Health and Social Services and the Office of Law Reform. The regulations and guidance in this series are primarily addressed to Health and Social Services Boards and Trusts. However, as they will have an impact upon the work of a wide range of agencies and individuals who work with children and young people in both the statutory and voluntary sector, they are of major importance to all involved with the welfare of children in any capacity including education and library boards, schools, those responsible for the management of children's homes and those providing child minding and day care services.

THE STATUS OF REGULATIONS AND GUIDANCE

*The regulations and guidance in this series build upon the legislative framework of the Children (Northern Ireland) Order 1995. The Children Order is law and must be complied with. The **regulations** made under the Children Order include permissions and restrictions as to what may or may not be done and also requirements on what must be done. As with the Order itself the regulations carry the full weight of law. The **guidance** issued under the Children Order is not law in the way that regulations are. Where the guidance explains the requirements of the Children Order or regulations it is reaffirming the law. Where it goes beyond regulations it conveys the message that "It is highly desirable to ..." or "Unless there is good reason not to, you should ..." rather than "You must". This is intended to give some degree of flexibility in the application of what the Department considers to be good practice. However it should be noted that whilst they are not in themselves law in the way that regulations are law it is possible that guidance documents may be referred to in court proceedings and that courts may expect justification for not following guidance.*

NOTE ON TERMINOLOGY

Although nothing in the Children Order turns on the sex of the person referred to, references in this volume to the child follow the legislative convention of the Children Order itself in referring to "he", "his" or "him".

CHILDREN ORDER

The Children Order includes statements as to the powers and duties of Health and Social Services Boards and Trusts. The Order itself uses the term "authority" to refer to a Board or Trust. The powers and duties will be exercised by a Board, except where a function is exercisable by a Trust by virtue of an authorisation for the time being in operation under Article 3(1) of the Health and Personal Social Services (Northern Ireland) Order 1994. In this series of guidance references are to a Trust except in the case of the registration and inspection functions in relation to children's homes described in Volume 4.

FURTHER READING

Whilst these volumes are designed to provide a comprehensive guide to the Children Order they do not purport to be a comprehensive survey of good practice.

It is suggested that reference might be made to:
The Social Services Librarian
Queen's University Medical Library
Institute of Clinical Science
Grosvenor Road
Belfast
BT12 6BJ

GENERAL PRINCIPLES ON WHICH THE CHILDREN ORDER IS BASED

In considering the detailed provisions of the Children Order in this volume attention is drawn to the major principles on which the Order is based.

- *The welfare of the child is the paramount consideration.*

- *Wherever possible, children should be brought up and cared for within their own families.*

- *Children should be safe and be protected by effective intervention if they are in danger, but such intervention should be open to challenge.*

- *When dealing with children, courts should ensure that delay is avoided, and may only make an order if to do so is better than making no order at all.*

CHILDREN ORDER

- Children should be kept informed about what happens to them, and should participate when decisions are made about their future.

- Parents continue to have parental responsibility even when their children are no longer living with them. They should be kept informed about their children and participate when decisions are made about their children's future.

- Parents with children in need should be helped to bring up their children themselves and such help should be provided in partnership with parents.

- Services provided to children and their families should draw on effective partnership between Health and Social Services Boards and Trusts and other agencies.

CHILDREN ORDER

VOLUME 1 - COURT ORDERS AND OTHER LEGAL ISSUES

The basic principles upon which courts must decide issues relating to the upbringing of children - *the welfare of the child is the paramount consideration, delay must be avoided and courts must be satisfied that making an order is better than making no order.*

New court arrangements for hearing public and private law orders. *Allocation, commencement and transfer* of cases and the appointment by courts of guardians ad litem to safeguard the interests of children.

The *meaning of parental responsibility - who has it automatically* and *how it can be acquired by unmarried fathers through the making of parental responsibility agreements or orders.* How third parties can acquire parental responsibility. *Sharing and delegating parental responsibility* and the responsibility of temporary carers.

Reform of the law on guardianship. All guardians, with few exceptions, will be persons who are not parents of the child. *Guardians can be appointed by a parent, guardian or by a court.* Guardians acquire parental responsibility when the appointment takes effect. Revocation, disclaimer and termination of guardianship.

New range of private law orders - *residence orders; contact orders; prohibited steps orders and specific issue orders -making arrangements as to a child's upbringing.* These orders collectively known as Article 8 orders. The orders can be made either on the court's own motion or on application in any family proceedings. *The meaning*

CHILDREN ORDER

*of "family proceedings". Those who can apply for Article 8 orders as of right and those who require the leave of the court. Restrictions on the making of Article 8 orders - the position of Trusts and Trust foster parents. The **relationship between Article 8 orders and public law proceedings and the need for Trusts to consider alternatives to care proceedings.***

Power of court to make family assistance orders. Purpose and requirements of the order.

Provisions of Article 15 and Schedule 1 regarding financial relief for children.

Duty on Trusts to investigate a child's circumstances on direction of a court or in specified circumstances. Purpose of inquiries and action following inquiries. Co-operation by other agencies.

*Applications for care and supervision orders - who may apply and notices. The **conditions for making the orders.** The matters to be considered when applying for an order. The duration of the orders and discharge of care orders and variation and discharge of supervision orders. The **duty to review cases of children in care.** Reasonable contact for specified persons will be allowed with children in care. Right of appeal.*

Circumstances where court may make an interim care or supervision order. Purpose and duration of interim orders. Courts' powers to give

CHILDREN ORDER

directions about medical examination or other assessment. Effect of interim orders on Trusts' responsibilities.

Prohibition against using the inherent jurisdiction of the High Court as an alternative to public law orders. Effect of relationship between wardship and Trust care. Power of the High Court to decide specific questions in relation to a child in care. Position of children in care who are made wards of court.

Duty on Trusts to promote contact between children and parents etc. Powers of court to determine issues involving contact and restrictions on contact. Powers of Trusts to restrict contact in certain circumstances.

Education and library boards may apply to the court for an education supervision order. The effect of education supervision orders. The grounds for the order. Consultation and co-operation between agencies. Applications to the court and reports. The duration of initial and subsequent orders. Effect on education supervision orders of other orders. Rights of appeal.

Purpose of emergency protection order and who may apply for an order. *Conditions to be satisfied before court makes an order. Effect of the order.* Application procedure. Powers of court to make directions including powers of entry. Removal and return of the child. Discharge of the order. Position of a child in a refuge.

CHILDREN ORDER

Power of court to make a child assessment order on application of Trust or authorised person. **Conditions to be satisfied before application is made or granted.** *Commencement, duration and effect of order. Court directions. Power of court to make an emergency protection order in place of a child assessment order. Need for Trusts to have regard to certain practice issues.*

Power of the police to take a child into police protection. Responsibilities of "designated officer". Parental responsibility. Trusts' liaison with police.

Unlawful removal of a child and offences. Circumstances in which court may make a recovery order. Purpose and operation of recovery order.

Restricting liberty should be seen as a last resort. *The* **criteria for restricting liberty. The maximum period without a court order,** *applications and the role of the court. The appointment of guardians ad litem and legal representation. The duration of first and subsequent orders. Rights of appeal.*

Transitional arrangements for court orders made on care, protection and control grounds under the Children and Young Persons Act (Northern Ireland) 1968 and private law orders.

Annex A   Main Court Structure

Annex B   Threshold Criteria for Care and Supervision Orders

CHILDREN ORDER

CHAPTER 1: INTRODUCTION

1.1   The Children Order brings together in a single coherent statutory framework most of the public and private law relating to the care, upbringing and protection of children. Briefly, public law deals with those areas where society intervenes (such as care proceedings) and private law addresses the behaviour of individuals towards each other (such as determining with whom children are to live following divorce).

1.2   The Order aims to strike a balance between the rights of children to express their views on decisions made about their lives, the rights of parents to exercise their responsibilities towards the child and the duty of the state to intervene where the child's welfare requires it.

1.3   The courts have considerable scope for discretion in their decisions about children. It is therefore important that practitioners in the field understand the broad objectives which the new legislation aims to achieve and the tools which it employs to do so.

Children and their families

1.4   The Children Order rests on the belief that children are generally best looked after within the family with both parents playing a full part and without resort to legal proceedings. That belief is reflected in:

(a)   the new concept of **parental responsibility**;

(b)   the ability of unmarried fathers to share that responsibility by agreement with the mother;

(c)   a Trust's duty to give support to children and their families;

(d)   a Trust's duty to return a child looked after by it to his family unless this is against the child's interests;

(e)   a Trust's duty to ensure contact with a child's parents, whenever possible, for a child looked after away from home.

CHILDREN ORDER

Paramountcy principle

1.5 In deciding any question about a child's upbringing or the administration of his property, the court must treat the welfare of the child as the paramount consideration (Article 3(1)). Article 3(1) is therefore of general application and is not restricted to Children Order proceedings. The paramountcy principle applies equally to care proceedings and emergency protection proceedings as it does to disputes between parents.

1.6 Although the scope of the paramountcy principle is wide it is not of unlimited application. It does not apply directly outside the context of court litigation and even where an issue is before the court it will only apply provided the child's upbringing or the administration of his property is directly in question.

No delay principle

1.7 The Children Order makes it clear that delay in court proceedings is generally harmful to children and should be avoided (Article 3(2)). Prolonged litigation about their future is deeply damaging to children, not only because of the uncertainty it creates, but also because of the harm it does to relationships between parents and their capacity to co-operate with one another in the future. The court is required to control the progress of individual cases and take steps to avoid unnecessary delay. To this end courts are directed in applications for Article 8 orders and orders under Part V of the Children Order to draw up a timetable and to give appropriate directions for adhering to that timetable.

1.8 Notwithstanding Article 3(2), it should not be thought that delay is always detrimental to the child's welfare. What has to be avoided is unplanned "drift". Delay which is purposeful, for example awaiting the outcome of an assessment, may be desirable. The principal effect of Article 3(2) is to place the onus upon the court to ensure that all proceedings concerning children are conducted as expeditiously as possible.

Welfare checklist

1.9 In contested proceedings for an Article 8 order (see Chapter 5)

CHILDREN ORDER

and in all care and supervision proceedings, the court **must** have regard to the following checklist:

(a) the ascertainable wishes and feelings of the child concerned, considered in light of his age and understanding;

(b) the child's physical, emotional and educational needs;

(c) the likely effect on the child of any change in his circumstances;

(d) the child's age, sex, background and any characteristics which the court considers relevant;

(e) any harm which the child has suffered or is at risk of suffering;

(f) how capable each of the parents or any other person in relation to whom the court considers the question to be relevant, is of meeting the child's needs;

(g) the range of powers available to the court under the Children Order in the proceedings in question.

There is, however, nothing to prevent courts from considering the checklist in other applications should the court choose to do so.

1.10 The checklist makes it clear that, whatever the order applied for in private proceedings, the court may make any other private order if it thinks it is best for the child, or may trigger a Trust investigation to see whether the Trust should apply for one of the orders available to protect the child. The full range of orders is available to a court hearing a Trust application for a care or other order in respect of the child.

No order principle

1.11 The Children Order requires that a court shall not make an order unless it is satisfied that the order will positively contribute to the child's welfare (Article 3(5)). There are two aims. The first is to discourage unnecessary court orders being made, for example as part of a standard package of orders. Orders should only be

CHILDREN ORDER

made where they are necessary to resolve a specific problem. This is intended to promote parental agreement and co-operation. The second aim is to ensure that an order is granted only where it will positively improve the child's welfare and not simply because the grounds for making the order are made out. The no order principle only applies where a court is considering whether or not to make one or more orders under the Children Order.

CHILDREN ORDER

CHAPTER 2: COURT ARRANGEMENTS

2.1   The Children Order paves the way for new court arrangements. It
       confers concurrent jurisdiction on the High Court, county courts
       and magistrates' courts and provides that a juvenile court
       (constituted under section 63 of, and Schedule 2 to, the Children
       and Young Persons Act (Northern Ireland) 1968) sitting to hear
       any proceedings under the Order may be known as a "Family
       Proceedings Court". The family business of juvenile courts will,
       so far as possible, be separated from the criminal business. The
       broad objective of creating a concurrent system of jurisdiction is
       to achieve as far as possible uniformity of orders, flexibility and
       consistency in procedures and remedies applying in different
       levels of court. Annex A at the end of this guidance summarises
       the main court structure in diagrammatic form.

Designation of courts

2.2   At the same time as conferring concurrent jurisdiction the Order
       also empowers the Lord Chancellor to provide that certain
       proceedings must be commenced in certain courts and in certain
       circumstances proceedings must be transferred to another court.
       That power has been exercised in the Children (Allocation of
       Proceedings) Order (Northern Ireland) 1996. The Allocation Order
       specifies seven juvenile courts as family proceedings courts.
       These are the juvenile courts sitting for the petty sessions districts
       of :

           Londonderry
           Ballymena
           Omagh
           Newry and Mourne
           Ards
           Craigavon
           Belfast and Newtownabbey

       There is one family proceedings court for each county court
       division and that court will exercise jurisdiction throughout the
       division in which it is situated.

2.3   As well as creating seven family proceedings courts at

magistrates' court level the Allocation Order also creates three family care centres at county court level. The three family care centres sit at:

Belfast Recorder's Court
Londonderry Recorder's Court
Craigavon County Court

Commencement of proceedings

2.4 Under the Allocation Order **public law applications** must be made to a family proceedings court subject to some minor exceptions. The exceptions are:

- if other public law applications involving a child are ongoing in another court then the application may be brought in that court;

- if the application is made as a result of an investigation directed by another court then the application may be brought in the court directing the investigation;

- where a parent has been prosecuted for failing to comply with a school attendance order the court hearing the prosecution may direct the education and library board to apply for an education supervision order and that application may be made to the court which heard the prosecution.

2.5 The family proceedings court will also hear **free-standing private law applications** (for example an application by an unmarried father for a parental responsibility order).

2.6 **Connected private law applications** will be made in the court where the main proceedings are to be heard. So if the parties are getting divorced in the divorce county court or in the High Court then any application with respect to a child should be made in that court. The same applies where there are proceedings between parents in the "domestic proceedings court" so that any application under the Children Order should be made to that court in the course of those proceedings.

Transfer of proceedings

2.7 The rules for transferring proceedings under the Children Order are governed solely by the Allocation Order. When considering transfer the court must have regard to the general principle that any delay in determining matters is likely to prejudice the welfare of the child. The court may therefore refuse to transfer a case, even where the relevant criteria are met, if this would unduly delay the proceedings to the child's detriment. The court must also consider what is in the best interests of the child.

2.8 A case which has been commenced in the family proceedings court must be transferred to a divorce county court or to the High Court if it appears that other proceedings relating to the child are ongoing in such a court and that it would be appropriate that all of the proceedings be heard together.

2.9 A case which has been commenced in the family proceedings court or a domestic proceedings court must be transferred to a family care centre if it is exceptionally grave, important or complex. The Allocation Order provides that a case may be considered exceptionally grave, important or complex because:

- of complicated or conflicting evidence about the risks to the child's physical or moral well being or about other matters relating to the child's welfare;

- there is a conflict with the law of another country;

- a large number of parties are involved;

- there is a difficult or novel point of law involved or there is a question of general public interest.

2.10 Where a case has been transferred to a family care centre on the basis that it is exceptionally grave, important or complex, the family care centre may consider that it is a case suitable for hearing in the High Court and transfer the case to the High Court.

2.11 Where the family proceedings court or the domestic proceedings court refuses to transfer a case to a family care centre because the court does not consider that it is exceptionally grave, important or complex, then either of the parties may apply to the family

care centre for an order requiring the case to be transferred. The Allocation Order also provides for a case which has been transferred to be retransferred where the higher court does not think it should have been transferred in the first place.

Appeals

2.12 Appeals from the seven family proceedings courts will lie to the three family care centres. Where a family care centre has dealt with the case on transfer from the family proceedings court (that is at first instance) an appeal from a family care centre lies to the High Court. Appeals from ordinary domestic proceedings courts will lie to the ordinary divisional county court.

Role of the guardian *ad litem*

2.13 The Children Order introduces a requirement for a guardian *ad litem* to be appointed by the court in most public law proceedings affecting a child. Guardians *ad litem* will also be appointed in all adoption cases. The guardian *ad litem* is an independent person appointed by the court to represent and safeguard the interests of children in "specified" proceedings. Specified proceedings are defined in Article 60(6) of the Children Order and further proceedings are specified in court rules.

2.14 The powers and duties of the guardian *ad litem* are set out in the Children Order and in two sets of court rules:

● The Family Proceedings Rules (Northern Ireland) 1996; and

● The Magistrates' Courts (Children (Northern Ireland) Order 1995) Rules (Northern Ireland) 1996.

The former apply to the High Court and county court while the latter apply to the magistrates' court (family proceedings courts and domestic proceedings courts).

2.15 The guardian *ad litem* is under a general duty to safeguard the interests of the child as prescribed by rules of court (Article 60(2)(b)). In fulfilling this role the guardian *ad litem* must bear in

mind the principle set out in Article 3(2) that delay is likely to prejudice the child's welfare. He must also have regard to the welfare checklist in Article 3(3). The guardian *ad litem*, unless excused, should attend all directions appointments and hearings of proceedings and advise the court on the following matters:

(a)   whether the child is of sufficient understanding for any purposes, including the child's refusal to submit to a medical or psychiatric examination or other assessment that the court has power to require, direct or order;

(b)   the wishes of a child in respect of any matter relevant to the proceedings, including his attendance at court;

(c)   the appropriate forum for the proceedings;

(d)   the appropriate timing of the proceedings or any part of them;

(e)   the options available to it in respect of the child and the suitability of each such option, including what order should be made in determining the application;

(f)   any other matter concerning which the court seeks his advice or concerning which he considers that the court should be informed.

2.16   Unless the court is satisfied that it is not necessary to safeguard the child's interests, the court will appoint a guardian *ad litem* in specified proceedings. The guardian *ad litem* will be appointed in accordance with court rules which provide that the appointment shall be made as soon as practicable after the commencement of the proceedings and his role lasts for the duration of the proceedings.

2.17   The guardian *ad litem* will play a full and active role, not only as representative and spokesperson for the child, but will, if appropriate, advise the court on matters such as timetabling and how to keep delays to a minimum in the interests of the child's welfare. The guardian *ad litem* is required to appoint a solicitor to act for the child, unless one is already appointed, and shall instruct the solicitor on all matters relevant to the interests of the child in the course of proceedings. Even in circumstances where a

child or young person is found to understand the nature of the proceedings and is believed to be competent to give instructions to a solicitor, the court still requires the independent view of the guardian *ad litem*.

2.18 The guardian *ad litem* must safeguard the interests of the child, taking account of the child's wishes and feelings, having regard to his age and understanding, and ensure that his wishes and feelings are communicated to the court. The guardian *ad litem*'s over-riding duty is to advise the court as to what is in the best interests of the child. In carrying out his duties the guardian *ad litem* will interview the child and others as appropriate and will have a right at all reasonable times to examine and to take copies of any relevant social services records pertaining to the child.

2.19 Guardians *ad litem* will be drawn from a panel of suitably qualified and trained persons. The Guardian Ad Litem (Panel) Regulations (Northern Ireland) 1996 provide for the establishment of a panel of guardians *ad litem* to act in specified proceedings. Responsibility for the administration and management of the panel lies with the Northern Ireland Guardian Ad Litem Agency which has been established by the Department of Health and Social Services under the Health and Personal Social Services (Special Agencies) (Northern Ireland) Order 1990. The agency has been established with the task of creating, organising and managing an independent GAL service for the whole of Northern Ireland. The GAL Agency is completely separate from both Boards and Trusts and is accountable to the Department of Health and Social Services for the performance of its functions.

CHAPTER 3: PARENTAL RESPONSIBILITY

3.1 The Children Order makes major changes in the private law relating to children. It introduces the fundamental concept of "parental responsibility". This is defined as **"all the rights, duties, powers, responsibilities and authority which by law a parent of a child has in relation to the child and his property"** (Article 6(1)). Parental responsibility is therefore concerned with bringing the child up, caring for him and making decisions about him. It does not affect the relationship of parent and child for other purposes. Thus, whether or not a parent has parental responsibility for a child does not affect any obligation towards the child, such as a statutory duty to maintain him (Article 6(4)(a)), nor does it affect succession rights (Article 6(4)(b)).

3.2 The importance of parental responsibility is emphasised in the Children Order by the fact that not only is it unaffected by the separation of parents but even when courts make orders in private proceedings such as divorce, that responsibility continues and is limited only to the extent that any order settles certain concrete issues between the parties. That arrangement aims to emphasise that interventions by the courts where there is family breakdown should not be regarded as lessening the duty on both parents to continue to play a full part in the child's upbringing. The following paragraphs set out the position regarding those who have parental responsibility.

Married parents

3.3 Article 5(1) provides that where the father and mother of the child were married to each other at the time of the child's birth they **each** have parental responsibility. The phrase "married to each other at the time of the child's birth", is to be interpreted in accordance with Article 155(2) and (4) of the Children Order. Read with Article 155, Article 5(1) refers to a child whose parents were married to each other at any time during the period beginning with insemination or (where there was no insemination) conception and ending with birth, and also includes a child who is treated as legitimate under a range of different statutory provisions, or is an adopted child.

CHILDREN ORDER

Unmarried mothers

3.4 Where a child's father and mother were not married to each other at the time of the child's birth, then only the mother automatically has parental responsibility for the child (Article 5(2)(a)).

Unmarried fathers

3.5 Article 5(2)(b) provides that a father who remains unmarried to the child's mother shall not have parental responsibility unless he acquires it in accordance with the provisions of the Children Order. An unmarried father may acquire parental responsibility:

(a) by subsequently marrying the child's mother;

(b) by applying to the court for **a parental responsibility** order under Article 7(1)(a); this places him in the same position as a married father, sharing parental responsibility with the mother;

(c) by making an agreement (known as **"a parental responsibility agreement"**) with the mother under Article 7(1)(b). Such agreements will have effect only if they are made in the prescribed form, and recorded in the prescribed manner (Article 7(2)). This is intended to be a simple method by which unmarried parents may share parental responsibility without going to court. An agreement has the same effect as an order under Article 7(1)(a) and can only be brought to an end by the court. If the mother and father are living together in a stable relationship when the child is born, and wish to share responsibility for bringing him up, it may be in the child's interests for them to make an Article 7 agreement. The mother may also feel that it is important for them to share responsibility in this way even if they are not living together. Where unmarried parents have reached an agreement, the father's position will be the same as if they had been married unless the court brings the arrangement to an end;

(d) by having a residence order made in his favour. In this case Article 12(1) requires that an order under Article 7(1)(a) is

also made. This is to ensure that a father who is entitled to have the child live with him under a court order will always have parental responsibility for him. If that residence order is later discharged, the parental responsibility order will not come to an end, unless the court specifically decides that it should (Article 12(4));

(e)   by being appointed as a guardian for the child. The cases in which it would be appropriate to appoint the father guardian are less common. The mother might wish to do this in case she were to die prematurely, but in that case she might be equally happy to make an agreement to share responsibility with the unmarried father during her lifetime. If the question of a court appointment arises after the mother's death, it would be more appropriate to make a parental responsibility order which recognises not only that he has parental responsibility, but also that he is the child's father.

3.6   Both an agreement and an order under Article 7 can only be brought to an end by a court order. Any person who has parental responsibility for the child (which includes the father), or the child himself with leave of the court (which may only be granted if the court is satisfied that the child has sufficient understanding to make the application) (Article 7(5)), may apply for the parental responsibility order or agreement to be brought to an end (Article 7(4)). Otherwise a parental responsibility order or agreement will end automatically when the child reaches the age of 18 (Article 179(7) and (8)).

3.7   An unmarried father who does not have parental responsibility is nevertheless a "parent" for the purposes of the Children Order. He has the right of any parent to apply to the courts for any type of order (Article 10(4)) and is entitled to reasonable contact with a child in care (under Article 53(1)). He is not, however, entitled to remove a child from accommodation provided by a Trust under Article 21, nor is his agreement required to the child's adoption.

Acquisition of parental responsibility by others

3.8   People other than parents may acquire parental responsibility. Anyone in whose favour a residence order has been made will

have parental responsibility for so long as the order remains in force (Article 12(2)). Any person appointed as a guardian (under Articles 159 and 160), on the death of a parent, will have parental responsibility. **A Trust also has parental responsibility while an interim or final care order or an emergency protection order is in force. It is important to note that in these circumstances the Trust will have parental responsibility for a child it has placed with a family or in residential care, even where the latter is provided in a voluntary or privately run children's home. A Trust does not acquire parental responsibility while a child is being accommodated by it under voluntary arrangements.**

Sharing parental responsibility for a child

3.9   Article 5(4) provides that more than one person may have parental responsibility for the same child at the same time. Article 5(5) makes it clear that neither parent will lose parental responsibility solely because someone else acquires it through a court order. This means, for example, that upon divorce a father does not lose parental responsibility even if a step-parent acquires it under a residence order. In this situation the mother, stepfather and father all share responsibility and, subject to not acting in a way that is incompatible with a court order, each will be able to exercise their responsibilities independently of the others (Article 5(7)). The sharing of parental responsibility is dealt with in more detail below in relation to the effect of residence orders (see paragraphs 5.5 - 5.10). Another consequence of Article 5(5) is that **parents do not lose parental responsibility when a Trust obtains a care order, nor when an emergency protection order is made.**

Independent exercise of parental responsibility

3.10   Article 5(6) provides that each person who holds parental responsibility may act alone and without the other or others in meeting that responsibility. **There is every expectation that those with parental responsibility will consult together and reach an agreement on any steps to be taken, but it must be recognised that there is no legally enforceable duty to consult.** Where one parent or any other person with parental

responsibility proposes to take a step which any other person with parental responsibility objects to, the latter may apply to the court for a prohibited steps order or in certain circumstances a specific issue order (see Chapter 5).

3.11 The ability to take independent action is subject to two restrictions. Article 5(6) provides that no steps shall be taken to affect the operation of any statutory provision which requires the consent of more than one person in a matter affecting the child and thus agreement to adoption, consent to marriage and consent to removal from the United Kingdom cannot be exercised without all those persons with parental responsibility giving their consent. The second restriction is that any step which a person with parental responsibility takes must be one which is compatible with any orders which have been made with respect to the child under the Children Order (Article 5(7)).

When a child is in care

3.12 The only exception to the rule which permits independent action to meet shared parental responsibility arises when a child is committed to care by a court. Here, a Trust is given power to determine the extent to which another person with parental responsibility may act (Article 52(3)(b) and (4)).

Delegation of parental responsibility

3.13 Informal arrangements for the delegation of parental responsibility are covered by Article 5(8), which provides that a person with parental responsibility cannot surrender or transfer any part of that responsibility to another, but may arrange for some or all of it to be met by one or more persons acting on his behalf. The person to whom responsibility is delegated may already have parental responsibility for the child, for example, if he is the other parent (Article 5(9)). Such an arrangement will not, however, affect any liability of a person with parental responsibility for the child for failure to meet that responsibility (Article 5(10)). **Thus, whilst the Children Order permits parents to delegate responsibility on a temporary basis, for example to a babysitter, it will be the parent's duty to ensure that the arrangements made for temporary care of the child**

are satisfactory. Failure to do so may render a parent guilty of an offence (of cruelty, neglect etc) under section 20 of the Children and Young Persons Act (Northern Ireland) 1968.

The position of those who have care of a child but who do not have parental responsibility

3.14 The position of the temporary carer is clarified by Article 6(5), which provides that **a person who has care of the child but does not have parental responsibility may do "what is reasonable in all the circumstances of the case for the purpose of safeguarding or promoting the child's welfare" (Article 6(5)).** This will cover actions taken by people looking after a child who is being accommodated by a Trust under Article 21, provided that these are reasonable in the circumstances. What is reasonable will depend upon the urgency and gravity of what is required and the extent to which it is practicable to consult a person with parental responsibility. Anyone who cares for a child is obliged by section 20 of the Children and Young Persons Act (Northern Ireland) 1968 not to assault, ill-treat, neglect, abandon or expose the child in a manner likely to cause unnecessary suffering or injury to health.

A person appointed as a guardian on the death of a parent

3.15 A guardian may be appointed to take over parental responsibility for a child when a parent with parental responsibility dies. A guardian may be any other individual (including a parent). The guardian acquires parental responsibility (if he does not already have it) when the appointment takes effect (Article 159(4) or 160(4)). See Chapter 4 for details about the appointment of guardians.

CHAPTER 4: GUARDIANSHIP

4.1   The Children Order replaces the previous law of guardianship. The object is now to provide someone to take parental responsibility for a child whose parents have died. The concept of parental guardianship is therefore abolished (by Article 5(3) and the repeal of the Guardianship of Infants Act 1886). All guardians will be non-parents, apart from those exceptional cases in which an unmarried father is appointed guardian instead of being given parental responsibility under Article 7 (see paragraph 3.5 above). A guardian must be an 'individual', ie a person rather than a Trust or voluntary organisation. Once the appointment takes effect, the guardian will have the same parental responsibility as a natural parent (Articles 159(4) and 160(4)).

4.2   A guardian may be appointed by any parent with parental responsibility, or by any guardian, or by a court. With one exception, however, a private appointment cannot take effect, nor can a court appointment be made, if the child still has a surviving parent with parental responsibility for him.

4.3   It will no longer be possible to appoint a guardian who is responsible for the child's property but not for bringing him up. There is a power for rules of court to preserve the inherent power of the High Court to appoint a guardian of the child's fortune or estate in certain exceptional cases where the Official Solicitor acts at present, for example in handling criminal injuries compensation for children who have been abused by their parents, but this has not been exercised at present (Article 159(5) and (6)).

Appointment of guardian by a court

4.4   The High Court or a county court can appoint a guardian for a child either on application or of its own motion in any family proceedings (Article 159(1) and (2)). However, the court only has power to appoint a guardian:

(a)   where the child has no parent with parental responsibility, either because both parents have died, or because the child's mother has died and his father does not have parental responsibility; or

CHILDREN ORDER

(b)   where, even though the child still has a parent with parental responsibility, the child's other parent or guardian has died and, immediately before the child's death, the deceased had a residence order in his favour in respect of the child (Article 159(1)); this is to cater for a child whose parents are separated when the parent with whom the child is living dies; but even then, if there is no court order providing that the child is to live with only one of them, the survivor will assume sole responsibility for the child.

4.5   No court appointment may be made under Article 159(1)(b) if the residence order in question was also in favour of a surviving parent of the child (Article 159(3)).

4.6   If either of the situations in Article 159(1) arises in relation to a child who is the subject of a care order, the Trust may wish to consider whether it would be in the child's interests for someone, perhaps a member of the family, to be appointed to take the place of the parent who has died. That person would share parental responsibility with the Trust, subject to the care order, and would be entitled to reasonable contact with the child under Article 53(1), to apply for the care order to be discharged under Article 58(1), and to withhold agreement to the child's adoption unless this could be dispensed with on any of the usual grounds. For some children this could be a valuable way of demonstrating the continued commitment and concern of their extended family, even if for the time being they are to remain in Trust care.

4.7   For a child who is accommodated under Article 21 when either of the situations set out in paragraph 4.4 above arises, it may be even more beneficial for a guardian to be appointed, particularly if the threshold criteria for making a care order do not exist. Even if they do, the Trust may wish to consider whether appointing a guardian would serve the children's interests better than making a care order.

Appointment of guardian by parent or guardian

4.8   Guardianship appointments may also be made by a parent who has parental responsibility for the child or a person who has already been appointed as a guardian (Article 160(1) and (2)).

An appointment must be in writing, dated and signed by (or at the direction of) the maker (Article 160(3)). If it is made at the appointer's direction, the making must be attested by two witnesses. This is to cater for blind or physically disabled people who cannot write, but not for those who are absent or mentally incapacitated. An appointment may be made in a will or by deed but does not have to be made in these ways.

4.9　Guardianship appointments will no longer always come into effect on the death of the maker. If, on the maker's death, the child has a parent with parental responsibility, the appointment will not take effect until that parent also dies (Article 160(5) and (6)). The exception to this rule is that if, on the maker's death, there was a residence order in his favour, the appointment takes effect immediately (unless the residence order was also in favour of a surviving parent of the child - Article 160(5) and (7)). Where a residence order was not in existence in favour of the appointer and a surviving parent, it is presumed that the surviving parent ought to be left to care for the child as he wishes. If the parent wants to seek the help or advice of the person named by the appointer, he may always do so. On the surviving parent's death, however, the appointed person becomes the guardian. Guardianship appointments may be made individually or by people acting together (Article 160(8)).

Revocation, disclaimer and termination of guardianship

4.10　Articles 161, 162 and 163 govern the revocation, disclaimer and termination of guardianship appointments. The basic principle is that any later private appointment revokes an earlier one made by the same person in respect of the same child, unless it is clear that the purpose was to appoint an additional rather than a substitute guardian (Article 161(1)). A private appointment may also be revoked in the same simple way that an appointment can be made either in writing which is dated and signed by the maker or at his direction (Article 161(2)). If the revocation is signed at the maker's direction, the signature must be in his presence and that of two witnesses who attest or by destruction of the appointment by the maker (or in the maker's presence and at his direction) with the intention of revoking the appointment (Article 161(3)). Any appointment made in a will is revoked if the will itself is revoked (Article 161(4)).

4.11 There is also a new right for a privately appointed guardian formally to disclaim his appointment by written instrument, signed by the guardian and made within a reasonable time of first knowing that the appointment has taken effect (Article 162). Regulations may be made by the Department of Finance and Personnel prescribing the manner of recording disclaimers (Article 162(2)).

4.12 Guardianship comes to an end automatically when the child reaches the age of 18 (Article 179(7) and (8)), whether the appointment was made by the court or privately. Any appointment may also be brought to an end by order of the court on the application of:

(a) any person, including a Trust, who has parental responsibility for the child;

(b) with leave, the child (if he has sufficient understanding); or

(c) of the court's own motion in any family proceedings (Article 163).

CHILDREN ORDER

CHAPTER 5: ARTICLE 8 ORDERS

5.1   Part III of the Children Order gives courts the power to make a range of private law orders in respect of children in "family proceedings", as defined by Article 8(3) and (4). The orders regulate to varying degrees the exercise of parental responsibility and are designed to create greater flexibility than the access and custody orders which they replace. They should also reduce the need to use wardship proceedings under the inherent jurisdiction of the High Court. **These orders focus on the child's interests so as to resolve specific areas of dispute rather than allocating legal rights and are designed to encourage both parents to maintain their involvement in the child's life.**

5.2   **The basis on which private law orders relating to children may be granted has been radically reformed, with improved legal standing for unmarried fathers as well as for relatives and other non-parents. They will be made principally in private family proceedings (eg divorce) but they may also be made, subject to a number of restrictions, in public law care proceedings. Indeed, it is availability of these orders in care proceedings which greatly increases the options open to the courts to make orders that best suit the needs of the child. Trusts will need to be aware of the range of private law orders available and the circumstances in which they are likely to be used to safeguard and promote a child's safety.**

Article 8 orders

5.3   Article 8 creates four new types of order: these are defined by Article 8(1) as follows:

"a contact order" means an order requiring the person with whom a child lives, or is to live, to allow the child to visit or stay with the person named in the order, or for that person and the child otherwise to have contact with each other;

"a prohibited steps order" means an order that no step which could be taken by a parent in meeting his parental responsibility for a child, and which is of a kind specified in the order, shall be taken by any person without the consent of the court;

CHILDREN ORDER

"a residence order" means an order settling the arrangements to be made as to the person with whom a child is to live;

"a specific issue order" means an order giving directions for the purpose of determining a specific question which has arisen, or which may arise, in connection with any aspect of parental responsibility for a child.

5.4 Any of the above orders, or any order varying or discharging such an order, is referred to in the Children Order as an "Article 8 order". The court will be able to make an Article 8 order either upon application or of its own motion (Article 10(1)(a) and (b)), unlike care and supervision orders which may not be made of the court's own motion, except on an interim basis (Article 57(1)). The court will also have power, when making any Article 8 order, to include directions about how it is to be carried into effect, to impose conditions to be complied with (i) by any person in whose favour the order is made or (ii) a parent or (iii) a non-parent with parental responsibility or (iv) a person with whom the child is living, to specify the period for which the order, or any provision contained in it, will have effect, and to make such incidental, supplemental or consequential provision as the court thinks fit (Article 11(7)).

Residence orders

5.5 The residence order, insofar as it determines with whom a child is to live, is similar to the custody order which it replaces. There are, however, two important differences. Firstly, because it is more flexible and will be able to accommodate a wider range of circumstances, such as various shared care arrangements. Secondly, because changes in the child's residence should interfere as little as possible in the child's relationship with both parents, each parent retains full parental responsibility and with it the power to act independently regardless of who has a residence order. The intention is that both parents should feel that they have a continuing role to play in relation to their children.

5.6 Article 5(4) provides that more than one person may have parental responsibility for a child at the same time. Article 5(5) provides that a person with parental responsibility for a child does not lose it just because some other person subsequently

CHILDREN ORDER

acquires it. Thus, the making of a residence order in favour of one parent does not take away parental responsibility from the other. Similarly, the making of a residence order in favour of a third party who is not a parent or a guardian of the child, does not take away parental responsibility from either parent.

5.7 Article 5(6) provides that, where parental responsibility is shared, each may act independently of the other in meeting that responsibility. It is recognised that the making of a residence order in favour of one parent may curb the other parent's ability to act independently as in practice the day to day care of the child is largely controlled by the parent with whom the child lives. However, when the child is with the non-residential parent he may meet his parental responsibility to the full, without the need for consultation with the other parent. The only restrictions on this are that neither parent may act independently in matters where the consent of more than one person is expressly required by statute (Article 5(6)), nor may either parent act in any way that is incompatible with any order made in respect of the child (Article 5(7)). Thus, for example, one parent may not remove the child from the physical care of the parent (or indeed any other person) with whom the child is to live by virtue of a residence order but could take the same interest as any other parent in his child's education.

5.8 By virtue of Article 12(2), the making of a residence order in favour of a person who is not a parent or a guardian of a child has the effect of conferring parental responsibility on him while the residence order remains in force. However, he does not acquire the right to consent or refuse consent to the making of an application to free the child for adoption or to the making of an adoption order, or the right to appoint a guardian. Where a residence order is made in favour of an unmarried father the court must also make an order under Article 7 giving him parental responsibility (Article 12(1)). This must not be brought to an end while the residence order concerned remains in force (Article 12(4)). Indeed, if the residence order is subsequently discharged the order giving the unmarried father parental responsibility will continue until it is specifically revoked. In such cases it will usually be in the child's interests for the father to retain parental responsibility in just the same way that a married father does.

CHILDREN ORDER

5.9 Another effect of a residence order is that no person may cause the child to be known by a new surname or remove him from the United Kingdom without either the written consent of every person who has parental responsibility for the child or the leave of the court (Article 13(1)). This does not, however, prevent the person in whose favour the residence order has been made from removing the child for a period of less than one month (Article 13(2)). There is no limit on the number of these short trips, however, and if the non-residential parent feels that the child is being taken out of the United Kingdom too frequently or that there is a danger of abduction he should seek a prohibited steps order.

5.10 A residence order may be made in favour of more than one person at the same time even though they do not live together, in which case the order may specify the periods during which the child is to live in the different households concerned (Article 11(4)). A shared residence order could therefore be made where the child is to spend, for example, weekdays with one parent and weekends with the other or term time with one parent and school holidays with the other, or where the child is to spend large amounts of time with each parent. Since a residence order only settles the arrangements as to where the child is to live, any other conditions that are needed must be specified separately by the court under its powers in Article 11(7). A residence order will lapse if the parents with parental responsibility for the child subsequently live together for a period of more than six months (Article 11(5)).

Contact orders

5.11 Although contact orders are similar to access orders, which they replace, the form of the order is different in that rather than providing for the parent to have access to the child it provides for the child to visit or stay with the person named in the order. The emphasis is thus on the child rather than the parent. The order may provide for the child to have contact with **any** person, not just a parent, and more than one contact order may be made in respect of a child. "Contact" may range from long or short visits, to contact by letter or telephone. It is anticipated that the usual order will be for reasonable contact, although the court will be able to attach conditions or make directions under Article 11(7) where necessary. Contact orders, like residence orders, will lapse

if the parents subsequently live together for a period of more than six months (Article 11(6)).

5.12 Contact orders under Article 8 must be distinguished from orders under Article 53 for contact with a child in care. Article 8 contact orders cannot be made if the child is the subject of a care order, because in this case the Trust has a statutory duty to allow the child reasonable contact with his parents (whether or not they both have parental responsibility), any guardian, and any other person with whom the child was to live by virtue of a residence order in force immediately before the care order was made. Article 53 contact orders therefore will only be made if it is necessary to limit, remove or define such contact, or to provide for contact with some other person.

5.13 An Article 8 contact order is a positive order in the sense that it requires contact to be allowed between an individual and a child. When the Children Act 1989 was implemented it was thought that a contact order could not be used to deny contact and to do so required a prohibited steps order. This reasoning was rejected by the Court of Appeal in *Nottingham County Council v P* [1994] when Sir Stephen Brown commented:

"An order that there shall be "no contact" falls within the general concept and common sense requires that it should be considered to fall within the definition of "contact order" in section 8(1)".

5.14 However in a subsequent decision, in *Re H (Prohibited Steps Order)* [1995], the Court of Appeal made a prohibited steps order against a mother's former cohabitant preventing him from having or seeking contact with the children to whom it was considered he posed a risk. It was held that this was the only means by which an order could be directed (and thus enforced) against the man. Butler-Sloss commented that had a "no contact" order been made it would have been directed against the mother who would thus have been obliged to prevent contact. That would have been inappropriate in the case since she neither wanted the children to have such contact nor had she the power to control it.

5.15 Whether an Article 8 contact order can be used to deny contact will be a matter for judicial interpretation. However, in light of the above decisions it would seem more appropriate to use a prohibited steps order to deny contact.

Prohibited steps orders

5.16 Both prohibited steps orders and specific issue orders are concerned with "single issues" and are modelled on the wardship jurisdiction. The purpose of the prohibited steps order, however, is to impose a **specific** restriction on the exercise of parental responsibility instead of the vague requirement in wardship that no "important step" be taken in respect of the child without the court's consent. It could, for example, be used to prohibit a child's removal from the country where no residence order has been made and therefore no automatic restriction on removal applies: or to prevent the child's removal from his home before the court has had time to decide what order, if any, should be made.

5.17 A prohibited steps order may be made against anyone irrespective of whether he has parental responsibility, but can only prohibit "a step which could be taken by a parent in meeting his parental responsibility" for the child. It could not therefore be used, for example, to restrict publicity about a child since this is not within the scope of parental responsibility. An order could be made against an unmarried father whether or not he had parental responsibility or against a non-parent, for example, to restrain a former co-habitant from contacting or seeking to have contact.

Specific issue orders

5.18 Specific issue orders enable a specific question relating to the child to be brought before the court. Orders may be made in conjunction with residence or contact orders or on their own. The aim, however, is not to give one parent or the other a general 'right' to make decisions about a particular aspect of the child's upbringing, for example, his education or medical treatment, but rather to enable a **particular** dispute over such a matter to be resolved by the court, including the giving of detailed directions where necessary.

Limitation on making specific issue and prohibited steps orders

5.19 An important limitation both on prohibited steps and specific

issue orders is that they must concern an aspect of parental responsibility. Although wardship will still be an available option in private disputes, the intention is that its use by individuals will be greatly reduced by the introduction of prohibited steps and specific issue orders.

5.20 Trusts' use of wardship has been severely restricted by Article 173, which provides that the jurisdiction cannot be used for the purpose of placing a child in care, or in Trust accommodation, or under the supervision of a Trust. Trusts will, like anyone else, be able to apply for specific issue and prohibited steps orders, provided that they first obtain the court's leave (see paragraph 5.30). This will enable them to resolve certain issues which at present can only be resolved by making the child a ward of court, such as whether or not the child should have a particular operation. They may arise where a child who is accommodated voluntarily by the Trust is felt to be in need of a particular course of treatment urgently and the parents cannot be contacted. If, in all the circumstances of the case, the decision is likely to cause controversy at some future date, the Trust should seek an Article 8 specific issue order. Trusts will not, however, be able to do this if the child is subject to a care order, as the only Article 8 order which may be made in such cases is a residence order (Article 9(1)). Nor can they apply for a prohibited steps or specific issue order as a way of obtaining the care or supervision of a child, nor to obtain an order that the child be accommodated by them, nor can a prohibited steps or specific issue order confer any aspect of parental responsibility upon a Trust (Article 9(5)(b)).

5.21 Similarly, a prohibited steps or specific issue order may not be made "with a view to achieving a result which could be achieved by making a residence or contact order" (Article 9(5)(a)). This is to avoid either of these orders being used to achieve much the same practical results as residence and contact orders but without the same legal effects.

The meaning of 'family proceedings'

5.22 The court may make an Article 8 order with respect to a child in any family proceedings in which a question arises with respect to the welfare of that child (Article 10(1)). "Family proceedings" are defined by Article 8(3) as any proceedings:

"   (a)   under the inherent jurisdiction of the High Court in relation to children; and

(b)   under the provisions mentioned in paragraph (4) [of Article 8],

but does not include proceedings on an application for leave under Article 173(2)."

The provisions listed in Article 8(4) are: Parts II, III, V and XV of the Children Order, the Matrimonial Causes (Northern Ireland) Order 1978, the Domestic Proceedings (Northern Ireland) Order 1980, Articles 4 and 13 of the Family Law (Miscellaneous Provisions) (Northern Ireland) Order 1984, the Adoption (Northern Ireland) Order 1987, Part IV of the Matrimonial and Family Proceedings (Northern Ireland) Order 1989 and section 30 of the Human Fertilisation and Embryology Act 1990.

5.23   Article 8 orders may therefore be made in most proceedings specifically relating to the care and upbringing of children, that is wardship proceedings, proceedings under the Children Order itself, including applications for care and supervision orders and adoption proceedings. It should be noted that for the purpose of making Article 8 orders, the definition of family proceedings does not include proceedings for emergency protection, child assessment or recovery orders under Part VI of the Children Order or proceedings for secure accommodation orders under Article 44, which is in Part IV. Orders may also be made in certain proceedings which are primarily concerned with disputes between adults but in which the interests of the children may be very important. These include divorce, nullity and judicial separation proceedings, maintenance proceedings in magistrates' courts, and domestic violence or ouster proceedings in both magistrates' and the higher courts.

Who may apply for Article 8 orders?

5.24   The Children Order distinguishes between those who are entitled to apply for any or some of the Article 8 orders as of right and those who may only do so with leave of the court. Article 8 orders may be made either on application or of the court's own motion under Article 10(1) in the course of existing family proceedings or, in the absence of any other proceedings, on a

freestanding application under Article 10(2). Article 10 sets out the three basic categories of applicants for Article 8 orders.

Persons entitled to apply for any Article 8 order

5.25 In the first category are people who may apply as of right for **any** Article 8 order. These are the child's parents (including an unmarried father without parental responsibility); any guardian of the child; and any person in whose favour a residence order is in force with respect to the child (Article 10(4)).

Persons entitled to apply for residence or contact orders

5.26 In the second category are people who may apply as of right for a residence or contact order (but not a prohibited steps or specific issue order). These are:

(a) any party to a marriage (whether or not subsisting) in relation to whom the child is a child of the family;

(b) any person with whom the child has lived for a period of at least three years out of the last five; and

(c) any person who:

(i) where the child is subject to a residence order, has the consent of each of the persons in whose favour the order was made;

(ii) where the child is in care, has the consent of the Trust in whose care the child is; or

(iii) in any other case, has the consent of each of those (if any) who have parental responsibility for the child (Article 10(5)).

5.27 Group (a) consists primarily of step-parents. "Child of the family" in relation to the parties to a marriage is defined in Article 2(2) as:

" (a) a child of both of those parties; or

(b) any other child, not being a child who is

placed with those parties as foster parents by a Trust or voluntary organisation, who has been treated by both those parties as a child of their family".

Children formerly cared for and maintained (ie privately fostered) may therefore be included. The term has the same meaning as in the Matrimonial Causes (Northern Ireland) 1978 and the Domestic Proceedings (Northern Ireland) Order 1980.

5.28 Groups (b) and (c) comprise people who have the consent of those whose rights will be affected if any order is made and who can apply whether or not the child is currently living with them. People who do not have the consent must have had the child living with them for a total of three years. The period of three years need not be continuous but must not have begun more than five years before, or ended more than three months before, the making of the application (Article 10(10)). The three months will give them time to make an application if the child is removed against their wishes.

5.29 Article 10(6) provides that any person who does not otherwise fall into either of the first two categories above is nevertheless entitled to apply for the variation or discharge of an Article 8 order if, either the order was made on his application or, in the case of a contact order, he is named in that order. In addition rules of court may entitle further categories of people to apply without leave (Article 10(7)).

Persons who must seek leave to apply for Article 8 orders

5.30 The third category covers anyone else who, with the leave of the court, may apply for **any** Article 8 order (although in the case of Trusts and Trust foster parents there are certain restrictions, which will be dealt with below). This enables anyone with a genuine interest in the child's welfare to apply for an Article 8 order and should avoid the need to use wardship.

The leave criteria

5.31 The child himself can apply for leave, which may be granted if the

court is satisfied that he has sufficient understanding to make the proposed application (Article 10(8)).

5.32 Where the applicant is an adult, the court must have particular regard to the following factors in deciding whether or not to grant leave (Article 10(9)):

(a) the nature of the proposed application for the Article 8 order (such as whether the application is a genuine response to the child's welfare);

(b) the applicant's connection with the child (does this justify the seeking of a court order?);

(c) whether the child might be harmed by the disruption which the proposed application could make to his life (perhaps because of the stress the proceedings will have on the person caring for the child);

(d) where the child is being looked after by a Trust, the Trust's plans for the child's future and the wishes and feelings of the child's parents. This factor will be particularly relevant where a Trust foster parent is seeking leave. It is important to maintain the confidence of the child's parents in the Trust's child care service and of the Trust in its ability to plan for the child's future (see paragraph 5.35 which explains the circumstances in which the foster parent may apply).

5.33 The requirement of leave is intended to act as a filter to protect the child and his family against unwarranted interference with their comfort and security, while ensuring that the child's interests are properly respected.

The position of grandparents

5.34 Although under the previous law grandparents had the right to apply in certain circumstances for access under Article 16 of the Domestic Proceedings (Northern Ireland) Order 1980 (which is repealed by the Children Order), it is not intended that they be included in the category of persons entitled to apply for an Article 8 order without leave. On the other hand, they are unlikely to

have difficulty in obtaining leave to apply so that their position should, on the whole, be better than under the previous law which did not allow freestanding applications by grandparents. Grandparents, however, like other persons, can apply as of right for a residence or contact order if the child has lived with them for a period of at least three years (Article 10(5)).

The position of Trust foster parents

5.35   Trust foster parents are subject to the additional restriction that they cannot apply for leave to make an application for an Article 8 order with respect to a child they have fostered at any time within the past six months, unless they also have the consent of the Trust (Article 9(3)). This means that Trust foster parents fall into four categories:

(a)   those with whom the child had lived for a total of at least three years during the previous five, who may apply as of right for a residence or contact order;

(b)   those who have the consent of the people whose rights will be affected by the order, who may apply as of right for a residence or contact order;

(c)   relatives of the child, who will need leave to make any application if they do not fall within the first two rules, but do not need the additional consent of the Trust; and

(d)   everyone else, who will need both the consent of the Trust and the leave of the court to make an application for any sort of Article 8 order; this restriction is to prevent applications by foster parents at a stage when the Trust is still trying to assess what is best for the child in the long term and also so that parents will not be deterred from asking for their child to be accommodated with a Trust foster parent if the need arises.

Restrictions on Trusts applying for Article 8 orders

5.36   Article 9 imposes a number of restrictions on the making of Article 8 orders, chiefly in respect of Trusts. Article 9(1) prevents

a court from making an Article 8 order, other than a residence order, with respect to a child in care. The making of a residence order, however, has the effect of discharging any existing care order (Article 179(1)). For those with parental responsibility, this remedy will be an alternative to seeking to discharge a care order under Article 58. Unmarried fathers who, without parental responsibility, cannot apply for the discharge of a care order, may nevertheless apply for an Article 8 residence order.

5.37 One effect of the restriction in Article 9(1) is that a court cannot make a care order **and** an Article 8 order. However, because the restriction only applies where a child is subject to a care order there is nothing to prevent a court from making a supervision order **and** an Article 8 order.

5.38 The Children Order draws a clear distinction between children being provided with accommodation by a Trust on a voluntary basis and children in the care of a Trust by virtue of a care order. Because of this distinction, Article 9(1) does not apply where the child is being accommodated voluntarily by a Trust under Part IV of the Children Order.

5.39 Article 9(2) prevents Trusts from applying for or being granted a residence or contact order. This restriction is intended to prevent Trusts from obtaining parental responsibility for a child other than by means of a care order, which will only be granted if the criteria set out in Article 50 are met. Furthermore, once a care order has been made in respect of a child, the court's private law powers should not be used to interfere with the Trust's exercise of its statutory parental responsibilities.

5.40 This means that if an individual is unhappy with the arrangements decided on by the Trust for contact with a child in care, he must apply to the court for an order under Article 53. It also means that not only are individuals prevented from applying for prohibited steps or specific issue orders as a means of challenging the decisions of a Trust with respect to a child in its care, but the Trust itself cannot seek guidance from the court on matters concerning the child's upbringing by applying for one of these orders once the child is formally in its care. Instead, the Trust will have to apply for leave to invoke the High Court's inherent jurisdiction under Article 173(2).

CHILDREN ORDER

5.41 However, a Trust will be able to apply for leave to make an application for a specific issue or prohibited steps order with respect to a child who is not in its care under a care order, whether or not the child is being provided with accommodation or other services under the Children Order. The court will have to consider the usual criteria for granting leave under Article 10(9), but if the action which the Trust wishes to take or prevent falls within the scope of parental responsibility, then a specific issue or prohibited steps order may be available and the Trust will not be able to invoke the inherent jurisdiction of the High Court.

Children aged 16 or over

5.42 Articles 9(6) and 9(7) provide that the court shall not make any Article 8 order which is to have effect beyond a child's 16th birthday nor should an order be made once the child has reached the age of 16 unless the court is satisfied that the circumstances of the case are exceptional. An example of exceptional circumstances might be where the child concerned is mentally handicapped. In such circumstances, an order may continue until the child is 18.

5.43 Article 8 orders not expressed to extend beyond the child's 16th birthday automatically end when the child reaches 16 (Article 179(10)). Where a direction is made, the order will cease to have effect when the child reaches the age of 18 (Article 179(11)).

Article 8 orders in adoption proceedings

5.44 Adoption proceedings are "family proceedings" and it is therefore open to the court to make any Article 8 order either as an alternative or in addition to an adoption order. Thus, the court would be able to make a residence order instead of an adoption order in favour of a step-parent, relative or foster parent, whenever this would be better for the child.

5.45 It is now open to third parties to apply, or at least to seek leave to apply, for Article 8 orders in adoption proceedings. Thus, for example, grandparents may wish to apply for a contact order on an adoption application. Technically, an adoption order

extinguishes any existing order under the Children Order (Article 12(3)(b) of the Adoption (Northern Ireland) Order 1987 as substituted by paragraph 140(1) of Schedule 9 to the Children Order) but the court would have power to make an Article 8 order of its own motion once the adoption order had been made. The same applies after an order freeing the child for adoption.

The court's duty when considering whether to make an order

5.46 The general principle set out in Article 3(5) that the court should not make an order "unless it considers that doing so would be better for the child than making no order at all" applies whenever the court is considering whether to make one or more orders under the Children Order and therefore applies equally to private and public law proceedings.

5.47 The operation of this principle will be particularly noticeable in divorce and judicial separation proceedings. Article 44 of the Matrimonial Causes (Northern Ireland) Order 1978 no longer requires the court to make a declaration that the arrangements proposed for the children are "satisfactory" or "the best that can be devised in the circumstances" before granting a decree. The parties still have to provide information to the court about the proposed arrangements but the court is no longer required in every case to approve those arrangements. Instead, the duty of the court is limited to considering whether it should exercise any of its powers under the Children Order. It may feel, for example, that an investigation and report by a welfare officer is necessary or, in a disputed case, that it should make a residence or contact order. Postponement of the decree absolute may only be ordered where the court needs time to give further consideration to the case and there are exceptional circumstances which make it desirable in the interests of the child (Schedule 9, paragraph 95).

5.48 There are several situations where the court is likely to consider it better for the child to make an order than not. If the court has had to resolve a dispute between the parents, it is likely to be better for the child to make an order about it. Even if there is no dispute, the child's need for stability and security may be better served by making an order. There may also be specific legal advantages in doing so. One example is where abduction of the

child is a possibility, since a court order is necessary for enforcement proceedings in other parts of the United Kingdom under the Family Law Act 1986. Under the European Convention and under the Hague Convention an order will be necessary if the aggrieved party is, for example, an unmarried father or a relative who would not otherwise have "rights of custody". An advantage of having a residence order is that the child may be taken out of the country for periods of less than a month without the permission of other persons with parental authority or the court, whereas without an order this could amount to an offence under the Child Abduction (Northern Ireland) Order 1985. Also, if a person has a sole residence order in his favour and appoints a temporary guardian for the child, the appointment will take effect immediately on that person's death, even where there is a surviving parent. Depending on the circumstances of the case, the court might therefore be persuaded that an order would be in the child's interest.

5.49 The welfare principle, set out in Article 3(1), requires that whenever a court determines any question with respect to (a) the upbringing of a child; or (b) the administration of a child's property or the application of any income arising from it, the child's welfare shall be the court's paramount consideration. Not all proceedings affecting children's upbringing or property are governed by the welfare principle. For example, it is expressly excluded (by Article 2(1) -definition of "upbringing") from applications for maintenance for a child. Also, Article 9 of the Adoption (Northern Ireland) Order 1987 provides that the child's welfare shall be the "most important" consideration. On an application for an order under Article 4 of the Family Law (Miscellaneous Provisions) (Northern Ireland) Order 1984 the welfare of the child is merely one of the factors to which the court must have regard. It does, however, apply whenever a court is considering whether to make an Article 8 order, regardless of the type of proceedings in which the issue arises. The child's welfare would, therefore, be paramount if the court were considering making an Article 8 order in, for example, adoption proceedings.

5.50 In determining what is in the child's best interests, the court is required, in all contested applications for Article 8 orders, or for variation or discharge of such orders (as it is in all proceedings for

orders under Part V of the Children Order, or for their variation or discharge, whether contested or uncontested) to have regard to the checklist set out in Article 3(3).

5.51 The checklist does not apply in all "family proceedings", but only in contested private proceedings under Part III and any proceedings under Part V of the Children Order. Thus, although adoption proceedings are "family proceedings", and therefore any Article 8 order **may** be made, the court is not required to have regard to the checklist and therefore is under no duty to consider what alternatives may be available.

5.52 Article 3(2) requires the court "in **any** proceedings in which any question with regard to the upbringing of a child arises" to "have regard to the general principle that any delay in determining the question is likely to prejudice the welfare of the child". This principle thus applies equally to private proceedings including those brought other than under the Children Order and public proceedings.

The relationship between private law orders and public law proceedings

5.53 Because the court is required to have regard to the statutory checklist whenever it is considering whether to make, vary or discharge an order under Part V of the Children Order, it must consider whether a different order from the one applied for might be more appropriate. Since care and supervision proceedings come within the definition of "family proceedings" in Article 8(3), the court has the power to make any Article 8 order as an alternative. Thus, for example, the court might decide, on an application for a care order, that the child's interests would be better served by making a residence order in favour of, say, a relative. The threshold criteria under Article 50(2) do not then have to be met. **It is important for those considering care proceedings to consider the alternative possibilities, and in particular the extent to which the child's needs might be met within the extended family, with an appropriate combination of Article 8 orders and the provision of services by a Trust under Part IV of the Children Order.** The range of Article 8 orders is extremely flexible, allowing the court to provide the child with very similar protection to that which is available in wardship.

5.54 The court may also make an Article 8 order as an interim measure when a care application is pending. Article 11(3) provides that the court may make an Article 8 order at any time during the course of the proceedings in question even though it is not in a position to dispose finally of those proceedings and Article 11(7) enables an Article 8 order to be made for a specified period. The court could, for example, make a residence order in favour of another family member, or a foster parent, until the date of the hearing and regulate the child's contact with his parents by means of a contact order or prevent it altogether by means of a prohibited steps order. It should be noted however, that if, pending an application for a care or supervision order, the court decides to make a residence order with respect to the child, it must also make an interim supervision order "unless satisfied that his welfare will be satisfactorily safeguarded without an interim order being made" (Article 57(3)).

5.55 Although application may be made under Article 58 for discharge of a care order, or discharge or variation of a supervision order, by any person who has parental responsibility for the child, or the child himself or the Trust supervisor concerned, those without parental responsibility, such as unmarried fathers and other relatives of the child, have no right to make such an application. They may, however, apply for a residence order which, if granted, would have the effect of discharging any existing care order by virtue of Article 179(1). Since a residence order not only provides for the child to live with the person in whose favour it is made but also gives parental responsibility to that person while the order is in force (or, in the case of an unmarried father, he will acquire it by virtue of a separate order under Article 7(1)), the continuation of a care order would be inconsistent with the making of a residence order. Equally, the making of a care order with respect to a child who is the subject of an Article 8 order will discharge that order (Article 179(2)) and the making of a care order with respect to a child who is a ward of court will bring the wardship to an end (Article 179(4)).

CHAPTER 6: FAMILY ASSISTANCE ORDERS

6.1 Article 16 of the Children Order empowers a court to make a family assistance order. It may be made in **any** family proceedings where the court has power to make an Article 8 order with respect to any child, whether or not it actually makes such an order. The power may be exercised only by the court acting on its own motion and must be distinguished from supervision orders made under Article 50. A family assistance order aims simply to provide short-term help to a family, to overcome the problems and conflicts associated with their separation or divorce. Help may well be focused more on the adults rather than the child.

6.2 The order will require a Trust to make a suitably qualified person available, "to advise, assist and (where appropriate) befriend any person named in the order" (Article 16(1)).

The persons who may be named in the order are:

(a) any parent or guardian of the child;

(b) any person with whom the child is living or in whose favour a contact order is in force with respect to the child;

(c) the child himself.

The order may also require any of the persons named in it to take specified steps with a view to enabling the suitably qualified person to be kept informed of the address of any person named in the order and to be allowed to visit any such person (Article 16(4)).

6.3 **A family assistance order can only be made if the court is satisfied that the circumstances of the case are exceptional (Article 16(3)(a)).** It should not therefore be made as a matter of routine. Furthermore, it will be particularly important in all orders for the court to make plain at the outset why family assistance is needed and what it is hoped to achieve by it. As the aim of the order is to provide voluntary assistance, it is also necessary for the court to obtain the consent of every person to be named in the order, except the child (Article 16(3)(b)). Since it is intended as a short-term remedy only, no order can have effect for a

period of more than six months (Article 16(5)), although there is no restriction on making any further order.

6.4　When both a family assistance order and an Article 8 order are in force at the same time with respect to a child, the suitably qualified person concerned may refer to the court the question whether the Article 8 order should be varied or discharged (Article 16(6)). A family assistance order may not be made requiring a Trust to make a suitably qualified person available unless either the Trust agrees or if the child concerned lives or will live within the Trust's area (Article 16(7)).

CHAPTER 7: ORDERS FOR THE FINANCIAL PROVISION FOR CHILDREN

7.1 The general power of the courts to make orders for financial provision for children who are not covered by the provisions of the Child Support (Northern Ireland) Order 1991 (and the subordinate legislation made under that Order) is contained in Article 15 of, and Schedule 1 to, the Children Order. Schedule 1 seeks to provide a single statutory scheme for financial provision for children and is without prejudice to the court's powers to make orders in matrimonial proceedings under the Matrimonial Causes (Northern Ireland) Order 1978 or the Domestic Proceedings (Northern Ireland) Order 1980. Where proceedings are exclusively concerned with the children, then parents, spouses or others seeking financial provision from either or both parents must do so using the statutory scheme laid down in Schedule 1. Where, however, the question of financial provision comes up in matrimonial proceedings, the courts may make orders under the relevant matrimonial legislation, which may be more appropriate where an adult is seeking relief for herself and the children at the same time.

7.2 The Children Order permits, in certain circumstances, children over 18 years of age to apply for financial provision from their parents (Schedule 1, paragraphs 1(1) and 3(1)). A "parent" is defined for the purposes of Schedule 1 so as to include any party to a marriage (whether subsisting or not) in relation to whom the child concerned is a "child of the family"; and for this purpose any reference to either or both parents of a child is to be construed as references to any and all his parents (Schedule 1, paragraph 1(2)). This means that a person may apply for, or be made to pay under, an order in respect of a child who is not his own, but who has been treated by himself and his spouse (or ex-spouse, as appropriate) as a child of the family. The only circumstances in which this definition of a parent does not apply is when the court is considering liability to pay maintenance beyond the age of 18 or where a Trust is considering making payment of a residence order allowance.

Applications for orders for financial provision

7.3 Orders for financial relief will generally only be made upon an application by parents (including unmarried parents), guardians or

CHILDREN ORDER

by any person in whose favour a residence order is in force with respect to the child (Schedule 1, paragraph 2(1)). However, the court can make a financial order of its own motion where it is making, varying or discharging a residence order (Schedule 1, paragraph 2(6)) or where the child concerned is a ward of court (Schedule 1, paragraph 2(7)).

Powers of the court

7.4 The power to order financial provision under Schedule 1 is vested in the High Court, county courts and magistrates courts. All courts may order the making of unsecured periodical payments, however the power of a magistrates court to order lump sum payments is subject to a maximum limit of £1,000 (although the maximum may be raised by an order made by the Lord Chancellor) (Schedule 1, paragraph 6(2)).

7.5 A lump sum order may be made to defray expenses or liabilities incurred in connection with the birth of the child, or in maintaining the child, which were reasonably incurred before the order was made (Schedule 1, paragraph 6(1)). The court may provide for any lump sum order to be paid by instalments, although where the court does so provide, the order may be varied on the application of the payer or recipient in terms of the number of instalments, the amount of each instalment and the date on which any instalment becomes payable (Schedule 1, paragraph 6(5) and (6)).

7.6 The High Court and county court possess further powers to order the making of secured periodical payments, settlements of property and transfers of property (Schedule 1, paragraph 2(1)(a) and 2(2)(b),(d) and (e)). Only one order for a settlement or for a transfer of property may be made against a parent for the same child, but there is no restriction on the number of periodical payments or lump sum orders which can be made in respect of a child before he reaches the age of 18 (Schedule 1, paragraph 2(5)). Schedule 1 provides that any order for secured or unsecured periodical payments may subsequently be varied or discharged upon the application of any person by or whom payments were required to be made (Schedule 1, paragraph 2(4)), or by the child himself, if he has reached the age of sixteen (Schedule 1, paragraph 7(4)).

7.7 All courts have the power to make interim orders for periodical payments pending the final disposal of the application (Schedule 1, paragraph 11). An interim order can require either or both parents to make such periodical payments at such times and for such term as the court thinks fit and the court may also give directions it deems appropriate (Schedule 1, paragraph 11(1)). The court cannot make an order backdating payments to a date before which the substantive application was made, although payments may be ordered to begin at a later date (Schedule 1, paragraph 11(2)). Interim orders will end either when the application is finally disposed of, or on such date as is specified in the interim order, although this can be varied by substituting a later date (Schedule 1 paragraph 11(3) and (4)).

7.8 Applications for financial provision are treated as "family proceedings" under the Children Order. The court therefore has power to make Article 8 or family assistance orders even though no application for such orders has been made and to direct an investigation of the child's circumstances under the provisions of Article 56.

Criteria to be applied when making orders

7.9 When considering whether to make a financial order under Schedule 1, the court must have regard to all the circumstances. The child's welfare is not the paramount consideration, although the presumption of no order applies so that an order may not be made unless to do so would be better for the child than not making it (Article 3(4)). The court must balance the interests of all those involved and, in particular, must consider (Schedule 1, paragraph 5):

(a) the income, earning capacity, property and other financial resources which each relevant person has or is likely to have in the foreseeable future;

(b) the financial needs, obligations and responsibilities which each relevant person has or is likely to have in the foreseeable future;

(c) the financial needs of the child;

CHILDREN ORDER

(d) the income, earning capacity (if any) and other financial resources of the child;

(e) any physical or mental disability of the child;

(f) the manner in which the child was being, or was expected to be educated or trained.

The relevant persons whose circumstances must be considered apart from the child are any parent, the applicant for the order and any other person in whose favour the court proposes to make an order (Schedule 1, paragraph 5(4)).

7.10 If an application is made against a person who is not the mother or father of the child, the court must also take into account whether that person has assumed responsibility for the child and, if so, to what extent, on what basis and for how long he has done so. It will also be relevant whether he knew that the child was not his child and what liability any other person has for the child (Schedule 1, paragraph 5(2)). It is further provided that where the court makes an order for financial provision against a person who is not the father of the child, it must record in the order that it has been made on the basis that the person concerned is not the child's father (Schedule 1, paragraph 5(3)).

Duration of orders

7.11 An order for unsecured or secured periodical payments may begin with the date of the application, or any later date but cannot in the first instance extend beyond the child's 17th birthday unless the court thinks it right in the circumstances of the case to specify a later date. An order shall not in any event extend beyond the child's 18th birthday unless it appears to the court that the child is or will be or, if an order were made, would be receiving instruction at an educational establishment or undergoing training for a trade, profession or vocation whether or not whist in gainful employment or there are special circumstances which justify the making of the order (Schedule 1, paragraph 4(1) and (2)).

7.12 Periodical payments orders which are not secured cease to have effect on the death of the payer (Schedule 1, paragraph 4(3)).

Any order for periodical payments (other than those under paragraph 3) ceases to have effect where the two parents who are payer and payee live together for a period of more than six months (Schedule 1, paragraph 4(4)).

Financial provision for persons over eighteen

7.13   Schedule 1 provides that a person over the age of eighteen may apply to the court for a periodical payments order and/or a lump sum payments order against either or both parents (Schedule 1, paragraph 3(2)). The court may make the order or orders if it is satisfied that the person is, or would be if an order was made, receiving instruction at an education institution or undergoing training for a trade, profession or vocation, or that there are special circumstances justifying an order (Schedule 1, paragraph 3(1)). An application may not be made for an order by a person, if immediately before he reached the age of sixteen there was a periodical payments order in force in respect of him, and no order can be made when the parents of the applicant are living together in the sane household (Schedule 1, paragraph 3(3) and (4)). A periodical payments order may be varied or discharged on the application of the person in whose favour the order was made, or on the application of any person by whom the order was to be paid (Schedule 1, paragraph 3(5)).

Financial provision for children resident outside Northern Ireland

7.14   Schedule 1 provides that a court can make orders for secured or unsecured periodical payments against a parent living in Northern Ireland where the child is living outside Northern Ireland with the other parent, a guardian, or a person in whose favour a residence order was in force with respect to the child (Schedule 1, paragraph 16(1)). The child cannot make an application himself but he may apply for a variation of an order when he has attained the age of sixteen (Schedule 1, paragraph 7(4)).

CHILDREN ORDER

CHAPTER 8: TRUSTS' DUTIES TO INVESTIGATE

8.1 A Trust is under a duty to investigate a child's welfare in a number of circumstances. The situations in which the Children Order imposes a duty on Trusts to investigate cases of alleged harm to children are set out in Articles 56 and 66 of, and Schedule 4 to, the Children Order.

Circumstances requiring investigation

8.2 A court in any family proceedings that comes before it has the power to direct a Trust to investigate a child's circumstances (Article 56(1)). A Trust has a similar duty to investigate:

(a) where it is informed that a child who lives, or is found, in its area is the subject of an emergency protection order or is in police protection (Article 66(1)(a));

(b) where the Trust has reasonable cause to suspect that a child who lives, or is found, in its area is suffering, or is likely to suffer, significant harm (Article 66(1)(b));

(c) when a court discharges an education supervision order and orders the Trust to investigate the circumstances of the child (paragraph 7(2) of Schedule 4);

(d) where an education and library board notifies the Trust that a child is persistently failing to comply with directions made under an education supervision order (paragraph 9 of Schedule 4).

Court directed investigation (Article 56 direction)

8.3 A court which is hearing family proceedings in which a question arises about the welfare of a child may direct a Trust to investigate the child's circumstances if it appears that a care or supervision order may be appropriate (Article 56(1)).

8.4 A direction requires the Trust to consider whether to take any action with respect to the child, such as applying for a care or supervision order or providing services or assistance to the child

or his family (Article 56(2)). If the Trust decides not to apply for a care or supervision order, it must report its decision to the court, giving its reasons and details of any action (including the provision of services or assistance) it is taking, or proposes to take, with respect to the child (Article 56(3)). This information must be provided within eight weeks of the direction, unless the court otherwise directs (Article 56(4)). The Trust must also consider whether the child's circumstances should be reviewed and, if so, decide when that review should begin (Article 56(6)).

8.5 Following a direction by a court in family proceedings, if the Trust decides to apply for a care or supervision order, it will usually make that application before the court which made the direction. While the Trust is carrying out an investigation under a direction, the court may make an interim care or supervision order to safeguard the child's welfare (Article 57(1)). This is the only circumstance in which the court may make such an order without an application by a Trust. The court must be satisfied that there are reasonable grounds for believing that the criteria in Article 50(2) are satisfied (see 9.18 below).

Child at risk (Article 66 investigation)

8.6 An application for an emergency protection order or a child assessment order should always be preceded by some kind of Trust investigation where the Trust is the applicant. Indeed the applicant is not likely to be able to satisfy the court of either set of grounds without being able to point to findings of an investigation, however limited this might be in some circumstances and especially in sudden emergencies. Action under Article 66 (the Trust's duty to investigate) should be seen as the usual first step when a question of child protection arises, and the guidance contained in the following paragraphs should therefore be read in conjunction with guidance on the protection orders.

Focus of inquiries

8.7 A Trust obliged to investigate under Article 66 must make whatever inquiries it considers to be necessary to enable it to decide whether it should take any action to safeguard or promote the child's welfare (Article 66(1)). Where a Trust has obtained an

emergency protection order with respect to a child the Trust must make (or have made on its behalf) the necessary inquiries to enable it to decide what action it should take to safeguard or promote the child's welfare (Article 66(2)).

8.8 The purpose of the investigation is to establish whether the Trust should make any application for a court order or exercise any of its other powers under the Children Order with respect to the child (Article 66(3)(a)). This refers primarily to the provision of services under Part IV of the Children Order.

8.9 It must be remembered that the right to apply for an emergency protection order is not limited to Trusts. In the case of a child who is the subject of an emergency protection order and who is not living in accommodation provided by or on behalf of the Trust, the inquiries should establish whether it would be in the child's best interests (while the emergency protection order remains in force) to be moved to such accommodation (Article 66(3)(b)). This will be particularly relevant where an emergency protection order has been granted to an applicant representing another agency, such as the NSPCC or to a private individual.

8.10 Article 66 imposes a positive duty on Trusts to make inquiries to see the child and to take legal action if access is denied. Under Article 66(4), a Trust must take such steps as are reasonably practicable (unless it is satisfied that it already has sufficient information) to obtain access to the child or to ensure that access to the child is obtained on its behalf by a person authorised by it for the purpose. These inquiries should be made with a view to enabling the Trust to determine what action, if any, to take with respect to the child.

Action following inquiries

8.11 Where, as a result of such inquiries, it appears to the Trust that there are matters concerned with the child's education which should be investigated, it must consult the relevant education and library board (Article 66(5)). This may include such situations as the child's non-attendance at a named school, the fact that the child is not registered at any school, or where the school raises questions about the child's behaviour.

8.12 Where, in the course of making its inquiries the Trust or its representative is refused access to the child concerned, or information as to the child's whereabouts is denied, the Trust must apply for an emergency protection order, a child assessment order, a care order or a supervision order, unless it is satisfied that the child's welfare can be satisfactorily safeguarded without an application (Article 66(6)).

8.13 If, as a result of its inquiries under Article 66, the Trust decides not to apply for any of the above orders, it must consider whether it would be appropriate to review the case at a later date. If it decides that it would be appropriate, the date on which that review is to begin must be set (Article 66(7)). Where a Trust concludes that it should take action to safeguard or promote the child's welfare, it shall take that action, so far as it is both within its power and reasonably practicable for it to do so (Article 66(8)). As a matter of good practice, where action involves an application for a court order and the application is refused, the Trust should consider whether and when to review the case.

Co-operation with inquiries

8.14 Where a Trust is conducting inquiries under Article 66, it shall be the duty of those agencies to whom Article 66(9) applies to assist it with those inquiries, in particular by providing it with relevant information and advice, if called upon to do so. However, this provision does not oblige any agency to assist a Trust where doing so would be unreasonable in all the circumstances of the case. What constitutes "unreasonable" will depend on local circumstances, and this will necessitate having good inter-agency liaison about what would normally be expected from co-operating agencies, and what could be done to resolve difficulties when they occur.

8.15 The agencies to whom this duty applies are any Board, any Trust, any education and library board, the Northern Ireland Housing Executive, and any special health and social services agency. The Department of Health and Social Services has a power to extend the duty to such other persons as it may direct (Article 66(9), (10) and (11)). Where appropriate, the Trust will also wish to consult with other agencies including the police and probation service, building on existing inter-agency networks and co-operation.

CHILDREN ORDER

Where a Trust is making inquiries under Article 66 with respect to a child who appears to the Trust to be ordinarily resident within the area of another Trust, the Trust must consult that other Trust which may undertake the necessary inquiries in its place (Article 66(12)).

CHAPTER 9: CARE AND SUPERVISION ORDERS

9.1   Under the Children Order compulsory intervention in the care and upbringing of a child will be possible only by court order. The proceedings should establish what action, if any, is in the child's interests, and the procedure should be as fair as possible to all concerned. The term "care" is used in the Children Order in relation to a child subject to a care order and not to a child accommodated by a Trust under voluntary arrangements.

9.2   A care or supervision order can be sought only when there appears to be no better way of safeguarding and promoting the welfare of the child suffering, or likely to suffer, significant harm. The Trust has a general duty to promote the upbringing of children in need by their families so far as this is consistent with its duty to promote children's welfare and to avoid the need for proceedings where possible. It should have regard to the court's presumption against making an order in Article 3(5) while at the same time giving paramount consideration to the child's welfare. This means that **voluntary arrangements through the provision of services to the child and his family should always be fully explored.** Where a care or supervision order is the appropriate remedy because control of the child's circumstances is necessary to promote his welfare, applications in such proceedings should be part of a carefully planned process. The new scheme imposes strict conditions which have to be met but does not place unnecessary obstacles in the way of action that is necessary to protect the child. It also increases opportunities to apply for discharge and variation of care orders and supervision orders.

9.3   There are common grounds for making care or supervision orders irrespective of the route by which cases proceed. These address present or prospective harm to the child and how this is occurring or may occur. Factors such as failure to receive suitable education and committing an offence will not be grounds in themselves for making a care or supervision order except in so far as they contribute to the harm done and may be attributable to lack of proper parenting.

9.4   The Children Order places greater emphasis on representing the views, feelings and needs of the child in these proceedings. Guardians *ad litem* must be appointed in most kinds of public law

proceedings where statutory intervention is sought under the Children Order unless the court is satisfied that this is not necessary in order to safeguard the child's interests. Where a guardian *ad litem* is to be appointed, the appointment should be made as soon as the application is received by the court or as appropriate and should help the court prevent unnecessary delay in dealing with the case. Where an application for a care or supervision order follows the making of an emergency protection order or child assessment order, a guardian *ad litem* will usually already have been appointed.

9.5   When a care order is in force the Trust and parents share parental responsibility for the child subject to the Trust's power to limit the exercise of such responsibility by the parents in order to safeguard the child's welfare, and to some specific limitations on the Trust. The Children Order also establishes a presumption of reasonable parental contact with children in care, subject to court orders and limited Trust action in emergencies.

Applications for care and supervision orders (Articles 50 and 51)

Order-making powers

9.6   The Children Order establishes that no child may be placed in the care of a Trust or put under the supervision of a Trust in civil proceedings except by action under the statutory scheme in Part V of the Order. There is one single set of conditions that must be established before the court can consider making a care or supervision order. Various routes into care or supervision under the Children and Young Persons Act (Northern Ireland) 1968 and other legislation have been abolished. So has the use of the High Court's inherent jurisdiction to put a child into Trust care (Article 173(1)), and the power of a court in criminal proceedings to make a fit person order placing the child in the care of a Trust. Supervision orders may still be made in juvenile criminal proceedings under the Children and Young Persons Act (Northern Ireland) 1968, as amended by Schedule 9 to the Children Order, but these differ in important respects from supervision orders made under the Children Order.

9.7   Care and supervision proceedings, and indeed all proceedings under Part V, are "family proceedings" (Article 8(3)), and for the

first time may be heard in the High Court and county courts as well as in the new family proceedings courts (Article 164(1)). Article 164(4) provides that a juvenile court exercising any jurisdiction conferred by the Children Order will be known as a family proceedings court, so that the family business of juvenile courts will be separated from criminal business.

9.8   The court hearing an application for a care order or supervision order may make any Article 8 order as an alternative to a care order or supervision order, or in combination with a supervision order, on application or on its own initiative. A court in any other family proceedings may also make a care or supervision order if the requirements of Article 50 are met either on an application following a direction to the Trust under Article 56 or on an application by a Trust or authorised person in the proceedings. This means a Trust or authorised person may apply for a care or supervision order in any proceedings under:

(a)   the inherent jurisdiction of the High Court in relation to children;

(b)   Parts II, III, V and XV of the Children Order;

(c)   the Matrimonial Causes (Northern Ireland) Order 1978;

(d)   the Domestic Proceedings (Northern Ireland) Order 1980;

(e)   Articles 4 and 13 of the Family Law (Miscellaneous Provisions) (Northern Ireland) Order 1984;

(f)   the Adoption (Northern Ireland) Order 1987;

(g)   Part IV of the Matrimonial and Family Proceedings (Northern Ireland) Order 1989;

(h)   section 30 of the Human Fertilisation and Embryology Act 1990.

9.9   In practice, the residence order is likely to be the most common of the Article 8 alternatives to care and supervision orders, albeit that a Trust cannot apply for a residence order on behalf of itself or a third party. Specific issue orders and prohibited steps orders cannot be used to achieve what may be achieved by the other

Article 8 orders, namely where the child should live and who should have contact with him (Article 9(5)), but may be used by Trusts in respect of a child **not** in their care, and others, to resolve other specially difficult matters which might previously have been referred to the wardship court. Contact with children in care is provided for specifically in Article 53.

Matters to be considered when deciding whether to apply for a care order or supervision order

9.10 Only a Trust or authorised person (as defined in Article 49(2)) may apply for a care or supervision order. At present only the NSPCC is authorised. It is no longer possible for education and library boards and the police to initiate these proceedings. The Children Order also repeals section 94 of the Children and Young Persons Act (Northern Ireland) 1968, which allowed a parent or guardian to apply for an order directing a Trust to bring a child before a juvenile court. The rationale for these changes is that it is the Trust alone which has statutory responsibility for investigating where a child is thought to be suffering harm, for promoting the upbringing of children in need by their families and for reducing the need to bring care proceedings.

9.11 This limitation places a special responsibility on the Trust. The Trust cannot expect to be sole repository of knowledge and wisdom about particular cases. **Full inter-agency co-operation including sharing information and participating in decision-making is essential whenever a possible care or supervision case is identified.**

9.12 **Trusts should in particular be guided by the founding principle set out in paragraph 9.2 in considering these matters. Having identified the child's needs, they should consider in each case whether any of the services which the Trust provides, or could provide, under Part IV and Schedule 2 (or which might be available from voluntary organisations or others) would be likely to improve the situation sufficiently. Where parents are struggling to care for the child, home-help, day care, parenting advice, voluntary befriending and other support of this kind, coupled with close monitoring of the child's welfare by a health visitor and social worker, or a temporary placement for the child in Trust accommodation under voluntary arrangements, may retrieve the situation.**

9.13 **The Trust should consider what the use of compulsory powers add in safeguarding the child and whether the gain is sufficient to justify use of compulsion and the trauma that may result.** Options should always be discussed with the parents or others having parental responsibility for the child, and with the child himself (unless very young) in language appropriate to his understanding. **Care or supervision proceedings should not be presented as a threat, but the parents should always understand where, in the absence of adequate parenting and co-operation, exercise of the Trust's responsibilities and duties will lead.**

9.14 Before proceeding with an application, the Trust should always seek legal advice on:

(a) whether, in the circumstances of the case and having regard to the Article 3(3) checklist, the court is likely to be satisfied first that the Article 50(2) criteria are satisfied and then that an order should be made under the Article 3(5) test;

(b) the implications of another party to the proceedings opposing the application and applying for an Article 8 order instead;

(c) whether the application falls within criteria of transfer of cases to a higher court and whether representations about this should be made;

(d) whether the court should be asked for an interim care or supervision order, the desired length of the initial interim order and what directions should be sought;

(e) the matters to be provided for in the Trust's advance statement of case, including copies of witness statements that can be made available and a broad outline of the Trust's plans for the child;

(f) notification and other procedural requirements and matters likely to be considered at a directions appointment;

(g) whether the court is likely to consider that in all the circumstances of the case a guardian *ad litem* does not need to be appointed;

(h)   whether use of a residence order linked with a supervision order would be an appropriate alternative to a care order.

9.15   An authorised person proposing to apply for a care or supervision order must, if it is reasonably practicable to do so and before making the application, consult the Trust where the child is ordinarily resident (Article 50(7)). The authorised person should establish from the Trust whether the child is the subject of any application or order specified in Article 50(8) ie an application for a care or supervision order which has not been disposed of; a care or supervision order (including a deemed care or supervision order under the Children Order's transitional provisions); a probation order under the Probation Act (Northern Ireland) 1950 or an order under section 74(1)(b) or (c) of the Children and Young Persons Act (Northern Ireland) 1968 (power of court to make fit person order or supervision order on finding of guilt).

9.16   As a matter of good practice, authorised persons should always keep the Trust informed of their concerns about children in the Trust's area, including any accommodated by the Trust, and share their information and thinking as matters develop and the need for intervention becomes apparent. They should seek to agree a course of action - for example, that the authorised person should proceed with an application or should modify it, that the Trust take it over instead, or that it be postponed pending further inquiries or other action. The Trust should look carefully into the authorised person's case, consulting other agencies and following the guidelines in paragraphs 9.12 and 9.13. It will be necessary to balance speed and thoroughness in making these inquiries in urgent cases. Having the matter out in court should only be necessary if there is a genuine difference of opinion between the Trust and the authorised person.

Conditions for a care or supervision order

9.17   No care or supervision order may be made with respect to a child who has reached the age of 17 (or 16 if married, for example where a child was married outside the United Kingdom). An application by an authorised person will not be entertained by the court if, at the time the application is made, the child was subject to an application or order specified in Article 50(8). These points should be checked by the Trust or other applicant as part of the process of deciding whether to apply. The court is likely to look

particularly keenly at a case for making an order for a young person who is approaching his 17th birthday (or 16th, if married). The order ceases to have effect at age 18 unless brought to an end earlier (Article 179(12)).

9.18 The court may not make a care or supervision order unless satisfied that (Article 50(2)):

(a) the child concerned is suffering significant harm, or is likely to suffer significant harm; and

(b) the harm or likelihood of harm is attributable to,

(i) the care given to the child, or likely to be given to the child if the order were not made, not being what it would be reasonable to expect a parent to give the child; or

(ii) the child's being beyond parental control.

These conditions are known as the threshold criteria. If satisfied, they indicate that an appropriate level of concern exists to justify legal intervention but an order will not automatically follow. The court then must go on to apply the child-centred principles of Article 3 of the Children Order, namely that the welfare of the child is the paramount consideration, the checklist of factors to be considered, and the presumption of no order. The court must also consider the wide range of powers available to it to make other orders, which include the orders under Article 8, and to give directions. Since proceedings under Article 50 are family proceedings (Article 8(3) and (4)), Article 8 orders can be made whether or not the threshold criteria are satisfied, and whether or not any party makes an application (Article 10(1)).

9.19 The threshold criteria in Article 50(2) replace the various conditions for a court order in respect of children in need of care, protection or control under the Children and Young Persons Act (Northern Ireland) 1968. The grounds in the 1968 Act were largely confined to an examination of present and past deficits in the development or well-being of the child. The new grounds are concerned with present or future harm: care or supervision should not be sought unless the child is currently suffering significant harm or would be likely to suffer significant harm if the

order were not made. Current or anticipated harm may have its origins in past harm, but there would have to be evidence of significant harm continuing or being likely to continue. Trusts will still, in exceptional circumstances and with the leave of the court, be able to invoke the High Court's inherent jurisdiction to resolve specific issues concerning a child in their care (Article 173(2)) (see Chapter 11).

9.20 Looking at the threshold criteria in more detail, there are two limbs and both have to be satisfied. The first focuses on present or anticipated harm. The second is that the harm, or likelihood of harm, is attributable to the parenting of the child or to the child's being beyond parental control.

Harm

9.21 " Harm" is defined in Article 2(2) as ill-treatment or the impairment of health or development. It is important to note that these are alternatives. Only one of these conditions needs to be satisfied but the proceedings may refer to all three.

Ill-treatment

9.22 "Ill-treatment" is defined, again in Article 2(2), as including sexual abuse and forms of ill-treatment that are not physical, as for example emotional abuse. It includes physical abuse by implication. Ill-treatment is sufficient proof of harm in itself and it is not necessary to show that impairment of health or development has followed, or is likely to follow, as a consequence, although that might be relevant to the question of whether the court should make an order. Thus, a child who is injured but has made a complete recovery, could be demonstrated to have suffered harm for the purposes of the proceedings.

Health or development

9.23 In most cases impairment of health or development is likely to provide the basis of harm. "Health" is defined in Article 2(2) as physical or mental health and "development" as physical,

intellectual, emotional, social or behavioural development. A child who misses education or who is failing to control his anti-social behaviour would come within this definition.

Comparison with "similar child"

9.24 Where the facts relate to health or development, it is also necessary to compare the health or development with what could be reasonably expected of a similar child. The meaning of "similar" in this context will require judicial interpretation, but may need to take account of environmental, social and cultural characteristics of the child. The need to use a standard appropriate for the child in question arises because some children have characteristics or handicaps which mean that they cannot be expected to be as healthy or well-developed as others. Equally, if the child needs special care or attention (because, for example, he is unusually difficult to control) then this is to be expected for the child. The standard should only be that which it is reasonable to expect for the particular child, rather than the best that could possibly be achieved; applying a "best" standard could open up the risk that a child might be removed from home simply because some other arrangement could cater better for the child's needs than care by the child's parents.

9.25 Having set an acceptable standard of upbringing for the child, it is necessary to show some significant deficit in that standard. Minor shortcomings in health care or minor deficits in physical, psychological or social development should not require compulsory intervention unless cumulatively they are having, or are likely to have, serious and lasting effects upon the child. Early intervention is always preferable but remedial action under Part IV of the Children Order or by health services is likely to be more appropriate.

Is the harm significant?

9.26 Whatever the nature of the harm the court has to consider whether the harm caused is significant. The word "significant" is not defined in the Children Order but some guidance is given. The Order states that, where the issue is harm to the child's health or development, then, in deciding whether the harm is

significant, the health or development of the child should be compared with that of a similar child (Article 50(3)). Drawing on advice as necessary, for example from the guardian *ad litem's* report or other expert advice, the court will have to establish what standard of health and development it would be reasonable to expect for a child with similar attributes, assess the shortfall in the health and development of the child in question against that standard, and decide whether the difference represents significant harm.

9.27 Where ill-treatment is alleged the similar child test is not appropriate and the court must simply decide on the facts whether the harm is significant. In ordinary use "significant" can mean considerable, noteworthy or important. The "significance" could exist in the seriousness of the harm or in the implications of it. For example, a broken leg would be a serious injury, but the implications of a small cigarette burn might be greater. This will be a finding of fact for the court.

Is the child suffering or likely to suffer harm?

9.28 The court must be satisfied that the child "is suffering, or is likely to suffer, significant harm". It is important to note that the conditions to be satisfied in the first limb of the threshold criteria relate to present or future harm. This allows proceedings to be considered where, for example, the child had suffered significant harm at some time in the past and is likely to do so again because of some recurring circumstance, as for example where physical abuse of a child is associated with bouts of parental depression; or where a newly-born baby, because of the family history, would be at risk if taken home; or where the welfare of a child who was being looked after by a Trust under voluntary accommodation arrangements (Article 21) would be at risk if the parents went ahead with plans to return the child to an unsuitable home environment. At the same time the conditions are intended to place a sufficiently difficult burden of proof upon the applicant so as to prevent unwarranted intervention in cases where the child is not genuinely at risk.

9.29 As mentioned in paragraph 9.28, the term "is suffering" refers to the present time. Although the threshold criteria will be a matter for judicial interpretation, the House of Lords has considered

CHILDREN ORDER

these words in the corresponding provision of the Children Act 1989 (section 31) in the case of *Re M (A Minor) (Care Order: Significant Harm) [1994]*. The central issue is whether the court can be satisfied that the child "is suffering" if he has been or could be removed from harm by the time of the hearing, even though there was harm at the time of intervention by social services.

9.30 In *Re M* the father murdered the mother. Their child went to live with a cousin of the mother. At first instance Bracewell J held that the criteria were satisfied and made a care order, although the child was to remain with the relative. The Court of Appeal held that if the arrangements with the relative were satisfactory, the criteria could not be satisfied. The House of Lords allowed the appeal against this decision. Lord Mackay said:

"There is much to be said for the view that the harm which Parliament contemplated was one which extended from the time the jurisdiction of the court is first invoked until the case is disposed of, and that was required to be done in the light of the general principle that any delay in determining the question is likely to prejudice the welfare of the child. There is nothing in section 31(2) which in my opinion requires that the conditions to be satisfied are to be dissociated from the time of the making of the application by the local authority. I would conclude that the natural construction of the conditions in section 31(2) is that where, at the time the application is to be disposed of, there are in place arrangements for the protection of the child by the local authority on an interim basis which protection has been continuously in place for some time, the relevant date with respect to which the court must be satisfied is the date at which the local authority initiated the procedure for protection under the Children Act from which these arrangements follow."

Is the harm attributable to care given or likely to be given?

9.31 The second limb requires the court to be satisfied that "the harm, or likelihood of harm, is attributable to the care given or likely to be given, to the child not being what it would be reasonable for a parent to give to the child". Harm caused solely by a third party is therefore excluded (unless the parent had failed to prevent it) and will require other forms of intervention to safeguard the child. The care given to the child has to be compared not with

what it would be reasonable to expect **the** parent to give to the child but with what it would be reasonable to expect **a** parent to give the child. It follows from "reasonable" in the text that the hypothetical parent would be a reasonable parent. The actual parents may be doing their best but are not able to meet the child's particular needs and are unwilling or incapable of making use of appropriate services. The standard of care which it would be reasonable to expect them to give may be very low. The court must compare the care being given to the child in question with what it would be reasonable to expect a reasonable parent to give the child, having regard to his needs. If a child has particular difficulties relating to any aspect of his health or development this could require a higher standard of care than for the average child. **The court will almost certainly expect to see professional evidence on the standard of care which could reasonably be expected of reasonable parents with support from community-wide services as appropriate where the child's needs are complex or demanding, or the lack of reasonable care is not immediately obvious.** "Care" is not defined but in the context of Article 50 must mean providing for the child's health and total development (physical, intellectual, emotional, social and behavioural) and not just having physical charge of the child.

9.32 The "likely" care element in Article 50(2)(b)(i) complements the "likely" harm in the first limb (paragraph 9.28). It provides for cases where the child's standard of care is deteriorating or the child is not, at the time of the application, being cared for by the parents but there would be reason for concern about the child's welfare if they started to look after the child again.

9.33 **Where parents fail to provide a reasonable standard of care it will be relevant to consider whether they could do so with provision of appropriate support services. Under Article 18 of the Children Order, Trusts have a general duty to provide a range of services to safeguard and promote the welfare of children in need and, in particular, to promote their upbringing within their own families. Where a child has particularly complex needs, a reasonable standard of care within the family may necessarily involve the provision of support services by a Trust. A Trust would be expected to offer these services before seeking an order unless it had clear evidence that the parents would be unwilling or**

incapable of making use of them. A reasonable parent would be expected to accept services offered for the child's benefit.

9.34 Where parents are not actually caring for the child at the time of the application the court must consider whether they would be likely to offer a reasonable standard of care if the child were returned to them. Their past and present behaviour will clearly be relevant together with any change in their circumstances since they last cared for the child.

Beyond parental control

9.35 The alternative causal condition in the second limb is that the child is beyond parental control. It provides for cases where, whatever the standard of care available to the child, he is not benefiting from it because of lack of parental control. It is immaterial whether this is the fault of the parents or the child. Such behaviour frequently stems from distorted or stressed relationships between parent and child.

Initial hearings: court requirements and party status

9.36 Court rules require the Trust or authorised person applying for a care or supervision order to serve a copy of the application on all the parties to the proceedings. The child and any person with parental responsibility for the child will automatically be given party status. The court may also direct that others be joined to the proceedings.

9.37 An application for a care or supervision order must be made on the prescribed form. Only one application form is required in respect of each family. The forms have been designed so as to encourage the preparation of documentary evidence and early advance disclosure of relevant evidence to the court and other parties. In particular the applicant for a care or supervision order will be required to submit details of plans for the future care of the child and any requests for directions, including restrictions on contact. The level of details given will be determined to some extent by the stage reached in the investigation of the child's circumstances. Any plan should be able to address the checklist of factors identified in Article 3(3) of the Children Order and why

an order is necessary, given the presumption of no order in Article 3(5).

9.38 The court will consider whether the proceedings should be transferred to a higher court according to the criteria set out in rules of court and whether a directions appointment should be held in advance of the first hearing. At a directions appointment, which may be held at any time during the course of the proceedings, directions may be issued on any of the following matters:

(a) timetable for the proceedings and directions to ensure the timetable is adhered to (this has to be done at some point in the proceedings, and the directions appointment is often the most convenient);

(b) the identity of the parties to the proceedings;

(c) the submission of evidence including experts' reports;

(d) the appointment of a guardian *ad litem* or solicitor;

(e) the date for a subsequent directions appointment, if any, or first hearing;

(f) the attendance of the child concerned;

(g) any other matters considered relevant.

9.39 Usually the court will not be able to decide the application for a care order or supervision order at the first hearing. The applicant should be ready to tell the court at the directions appointment:

(a) whether he is applying for an interim order and, if so, any directions under Article 57(6) relating to medical or psychiatric examination or any other kind of assessment (the power to order an examination or assessment relates to the child only);

(b) what plans the Trust has made for safeguarding and promoting the child's welfare while the interim order is in force and, where an interim care order is sought, what type of placement is envisaged;

(c)   in the case of an interim order, what proposals the Trust has for allowing the child reasonable contact with his parents and others under Article 53.

Timetable requirements (Article 51)

9.40   It must be expected that the court hearing an application for a care or supervision order will normally need to adjourn the proceedings to a further hearing or hearings because it is not in a position to decide the application, even when it is not contested. The guardian *ad litem* will usually need time to make inquiries, establish the child's and others' views, investigate the applicant's plans and prepare a report and recommendations for the court. Other parties will need to prepare their case, instruct a solicitor where appropriate, obtain witness statements etc. The Children Order and rules of court allow for these requirements but make specific provisions designed to ensure that applications are dealt with as soon as possible. These start with the principle in Article 3(2) that any delay in determining a question about the upbringing of a child is likely to prejudice his welfare.

9.41   Article 51(1) requires a court hearing an application under Part V of the Children Order to draw up a timetable with a view to disposing of the application without delay, and to give such directions as it considers appropriate for the purpose of ensuring, so far as reasonably practicable, that the timetable is adhered to. There are corresponding provisions in Article 11(1) and rules for proceedings where an Article 8 order is being considered.

9.42   Keeping to a minimum the number of adjournments and the length of intervals between hearings is a major objective of the Children Order. The court will be expected to recognise the urgency of care and supervision proceedings and organise its domestic business accordingly, to examine possible delays at preliminary hearings, avoid slack in directions on timetabling, and, with assistance from the guardian *ad litem*, monitor compliance with directions and the progress of the case.

9.43   Rules of court require guardians *ad litem* to assist and advise the court as to the timing of all or any part of the proceedings. The timetable should encourage expeditious handling of matters before the court whilst not discouraging sensible negotiations

between the parties. Delay is ordinarily harmful to the welfare of the child but planned and purposeful delay may be beneficial. The Trust should ensure that all staff concerned with a case before the court, including Trust legal staff and staff of other Trusts and agencies who may be involved, are made aware of court directions on timetabling and do whatever is necessary to ensure compliance with those directions. The applicant for the order should regard it as part of his responsibilities to help both the court clerk and the guardian *ad litem* identify and deal with difficulties likely to cause delay.

9.44　The court may make an interim care order or interim supervision order in the circumstances described in paragraph 10.1. Where it does so, the court can be expected to match the duration of the interim order to the adjournment period, having regard to the limits on length of interim orders in Article 57.

Effect of care orders

9.45　Article 52 of the Children Order defines the legal effect of a care order (including, by virtue of Article 49(1), an interim care order), whether made in care proceedings or in other family proceedings. It clarifies the relationship between a Trust's and parents' responsibilities for the child in care, and establishes a legal foundation for the Trust's welfare responsibilities towards children in care under Part IV of the Children Order. The effects of the making of a care order on other orders are set out in Article 179.

9.46　A care order places a child in the care of a designated Trust which must then receive and keep the child in care while the order remains in force (Article 52(1)). The Trust named must be the Trust in whose area the child is ordinarily resident. Where the child does not reside in the area of a Trust the order must name the Trust in whose area any circumstances arose in consequence of which the order is made (Article 50(9)). The Trust designated by the care order is responsible for looking after the child. It must provide accommodation for the child and maintain the child in accordance with Article 27; safeguard and promote the child's welfare (Article 26(1)(a)); and give effect to, or act in accordance with, the other welfare responsibilities in Part IV of the Children Order.

9.47 The designated Trust acquires parental responsibility for the child for as long as the order is in force, but the parent does not cease to have parental responsibility solely because some other person acquires it (Article 5(5)). It does have power to determine the extent to which parents or guardians (who do not lose their parental responsibility on the making of the order) may meet their responsibility. This power marks the principal difference in the positions on parental responsibility under a care order and a residence order (Article 12). It allows the Trust to deal with any conflict that may arise between the Trust and the parents in exercising their respective parental responsibilities.

9.48 Article 5(6) allows any person with parental responsibility to act alone and without others in meeting that responsibility. This is subject to the caveat in Article 5(7) that a person with parental responsibility may not act in a way which would be incompatible with an order made under the Children Order. However, there could be arguments as to whether a proposed action of which the Trust disapproved was incompatible with the care order. Article 52(3)(b) provides the Trust with the power to determine the extent to which a parent or guardian may meet his parental responsibility but only insofar as it is satisfied that it is necessary to do so in order to safeguard or promote the child's welfare. Where a Trust intends to limit the way in which a parent meets his responsibility this should be discussed with the parent and incorporated in the plan of arrangements for the child whilst in care so that it may be subject to periodic review. Note that exercising this power does not prevent a parent or guardian who has care of the child on a weekend visit, for example, from doing what is reasonable to safeguard or promote the child's welfare (Article 52(5)).

9.49 A parent or guardian also retains any rights, duties, powers, responsibilities or authority in relation to the child and his property which they have under other legislation (Article 52(9)). These include: the right to consent or refuse to consent to the child's marriage, rights under the Education and Libraries (Northern Ireland) Order 1986 in relation to the child's special educational needs, financial responsibility for the child and also some responsibility for the child's acts if he is in the parent's charge. However, under amendments to the Marriage Act (Northern Ireland) 1954 , a Trust's consent for the marriage of a child in care who is 16 or 17 is needed. A parent has no liability

to contribute towards the maintenance of a child looked after by a Trust if the parent is in receipt of specified benefits (Article 39(4)).

9.50 Subject to the specific restrictions in Article 52 (see below), a Trust has all the rights, duties, powers, responsibilities and authority to act as parent of the child in care and to discharge all its responsibilities to the child positively and effectively. These include having to decide how to best care for the child in accordance with Article 52. It may not transfer any part of its parental responsibility to someone else, but can arrange for some or all of it to be met on its behalf by others (eg a foster parent or a voluntary organisation).

9.51 Article 52 prevents a Trust doing certain things by virtue of its parental responsibility. It must not cause the child to be brought up in any religious persuasion other than that in which he would have been brought up had the order not been made. This does not prevent the child determining his own religious beliefs as he grows older; it simply requires the Trust not to bring about any change by its own action or inaction. A Trust should not, for example, place a child who has been brought up in a particular religion with a foster parent who, deliberately or by omission, would be likely to prevent the child continuing to practice his beliefs.

9.52 A Trust may not consent, or refuse to consent, to the making of an application for a freeing for adoption order; or to agree, or refuse to agree, to an adoption order or a proposed foreign adoption order. A Trust may not appoint a guardian for a child, which must always be done in accordance with Articles 159 and 160 of the Children Order.

9.53 A Trust may not change the child's surname or remove the child from the United Kingdom without either the written consent of every person with parental responsibility for the child, or the leave of the court. The restriction on removal does not apply where it is for less than one month (for example, to allow the child to go on holiday abroad with his foster parents or to visit relatives abroad), or to arrangements for the child to live permanently outside Northern Ireland approved by the court under Article 33.

9.54 A care order lasts until the child is 18, unless it is brought to an

end by a residence order (Article 179(1)), or by its discharge under Article 58. The making of an adoption or freeing for adoption order extinguishes any order under the Children Order (Articles 12(3) and 17(3) of the Adoption (Northern Ireland) Order 1987 as amended by paragraphs 140(1) and 143(2) of Schedule 9 to the Children Order).

9.55 Under Article 179, the making of a care order discharges any Article 8 order (including a residence order), supervision order or school attendance order to which the child was subject at the time the care order was made. It also brings any wardship to an end. If an emergency protection order is made while the child is subject to a care order, the care order will be superseded by the emergency protection order to allow the holder of the emergency protection order to take whatever action he considers necessary to protect the child. This may be necessary if a serious situation arises during a placement. However as a Trust has parental responsibility for the child by virtue of the care order, it is unlikely that this situation will arise very often. Before allowing an application, from whatever source, the court will wish to have regard to the existence of the care order.

Supervision orders

9.56 Supervision orders and interim supervision orders have for the most part been dealt with in the preceding paragraphs of this guidance - those on the court's order-making powers, applications, criteria for orders, court directions and variation and discharge of orders, for example - where the provisions are common to both supervision orders and care orders or raise common points. The following paragraphs deal more specifically with supervision orders and Article 54 of, and Schedule 3 to, the Children Order.

Duties of supervisor

9.57 A supervision order puts the child under the supervision of a designated Trust. The court cannot designate a Trust unless the Trust agrees or the child lives, or will live in its area (paragraph 8 of Schedule 3). The supervisor is given three specific duties in Article 54:

(a)   to advise, assist and befriend the child;

(b)   to take all reasonable steps to see that the order is given effect; and

(c)   to consider whether to apply for variation or discharge of the order where it is not being wholly complied with or he considers that the order may no longer be necessary.

The supervisor must also refer back to the court on medical treatment in accordance with paragraph 5(7) of Schedule 3 should the need arise.

9.58   A supervision order may require the child to:

(a)   live at a place specified in directions given by the supervisor;

(b)   take part in education or training activities;

(c)   report to particular places at particular times;

(d)   submit to psychiatric or medical examination or treatment (under court directions in the case of an interim supervision order, if this is required for health and development and/or evidential purposes);

(e)   be available for monitoring visits by the supervisor at the place where he is living.

It should be noted that the court cannot make a direction requiring the child to submit to psychiatric or medical examination or treatment unless the child, if of sufficient understanding to do so, consents to its inclusion in the order. A Trust should always consider very carefully when contemplating an application under Article 50 whether these powers, including the power of the court and supervisor to impose requirements on a responsible person or persons, are sufficient to promote and safeguard the welfare of the child. The court and guardian *ad litem* will certainly wish to do so. In this context a responsible person means any person with parental responsibility for the child, or any other person with whom the child is living (paragraph 1 of Schedule 3).

9.59 The requirements which may be made of the supervised child or responsible person are set out in detail in Schedule 3. Requirements as to treatment are wholly the responsibility of the court and have to be specified in the order itself (paragraph 5 of Schedule 3). Requirements as to examinations may be specified by the court in the order or by the supervisor (paragraph 4 of Schedule 3). Other matters are for the supervisor, provided the supervision order contains the necessary authority.

Power to give directions to the child

9.60 An order may require a child to comply with any directions given by the supervisor as to where the child should live, on reporting to a person and place and on participating in activities (paragraph 2 of Schedule 3). It is left to the supervisor to specify how and to what extent a child shall live away from home or participate in any activities under this provision.

Directions to the responsible person

9.61 The court may include a requirement that the person responsible for the child take steps to ensure that the child complies with the supervisor's directions (paragraph 3(1)(c) of Schedule 3). The court may take the view that the responsible person needs to participate in certain activities with the child or on his own. In this case it can include a requirement in the order that he comply with the supervisor's directions to attend at a specified place to participate in specified activities either with or without the child. The court can also require the responsible person through the supervision order to take all reasonable steps to ensure that the child complies with requirements and directions under paragraphs 4 and 5 of Schedule 3. The responsible person has to consent to requirements of himself being included in the order; the co-operation of the responsible person is a vital contribution to the effectiveness of the order.

Information

9.62 An order may require a child to keep the supervisor informed of any change of address (paragraph 7(1)(a) of Schedule 3). In addition, any person with parental responsibility for the child

must, on request, inform the supervisor of the child's address if known. This also applies to any person with whom the child is living (paragraph 7(2)(a) of Schedule 3).

Access to the child

9.63 An order may require a child to allow the supervisor to visit him at the place where he is living (paragraph 7(1)(b) of Schedule 3). In addition, the person with whom the child is living must allow the supervisor reasonable contact with the child (paragraph 7(2)(b) of Schedule 3).

Psychiatric and medical examinations/treatment

9.64 Paragraphs 4 and 5 of Schedule 3 deal with the important questions of health examinations and treatment at some length. The child may be required to submit to a medical or psychiatric examination by the court through the order or by direction of the supervisor if the order gives authority for this. The arrangements for the examination must be in accordance with paragraph 4(2) and (3) of Schedule 3. It may be carried out at a hospital with the child attending as a resident patient only if the court is satisfied by medical evidence that the child requires treatment and may be susceptible to it, and that it is necessary for the child to stay as a resident patient. The court must in all cases be satisfied that, if the child is of sufficient understanding to make an informed decision, he consents to the inclusion of these requirements, and that the arrangements will be satisfactory.

9.65 Paragraph 5 of Schedule 3 (psychiatric and medical treatment) requires all directions to be given by the court, not the supervisor, and it imposes different conditions for directions on psychiatric treatment (paragraph 5(1) and (2)) and physical treatment (paragraph 5(3) and (4)). In relation to physical treatment, the court has to be satisfied, on the basis of advice from a medical practitioner, that the treatment is needed and it must specify in the order the period of treatment and whether the child is to be an in-patient or out-patient. The same requirements regarding consent apply in the case of treatment as apply to examination. If the child is of sufficient understanding he must consent to the inclusion of the direction in the order. The same conditions apply to psychiatric treatment except that

the medical practitioner must be appointed under Part II of the Mental Health (Northern Ireland) Order 1986 and the court must be satisfied that the child's condition does not warrant detention under the Mental Health Order.

9.66 The medical practitioner responsible for the treatment must report in writing to the supervisor if he is unwilling for the treatment to continue for any reason, or if it is considered that the treatment should continue beyond the period specified, the child needs different treatment, the child is not susceptible to treatment or does not require further treatment. The supervisor must refer the report to the court, which may then cancel or vary its requirements as to treatment.

Discharge and variation

9.67 There is no prescribed remedy for breach of a requirement or direction; the supervisor would have to consider, where the order is not wholly complied with, whether to apply to the court for its variation or discharge (Article 54(1)(c)). If the supervisor is prevented from visiting the child or having reasonable contact with the child under paragraph 7(1)(b) and (2)(b) of Schedule 3, the supervisor may apply to the court for a warrant under Article 178. If the supervisor considers that the refusal of reasonable contact requires that urgent action be taken, the supervisor should consider whether to apply for an emergency protection order or ask a constable to take the child into police protection under Article 65.

9.68 Failure to comply with requirements may lead to a Trust reconsidering its plans for the child, and this possibility should be explained to the child, the responsible person and the child's parents, and to any other person caring for the child, so that they know where they stand and can see the value to the child of their co-operation. A Trust should at all times respond to non co-operation in a positive and constructive way designed to regain that co-operation. Failure to work closely with those concerned with the child's welfare, in particular with the parents, may lead to a breakdown in the Trust's relationship with the parents, and consequent harmful effects on the welfare of the child. The aim must be at all times to strive to gain the parents' support for the plans for the child's future. The court and guardian *ad litem* are

CHILDREN ORDER

also likely to want to ensure that the child and other persons understand the significance of the order when it is made.

Duration and extension of orders

9.69 Subject to its not being brought to an end earlier, a supervision order will last for one year in the first instance beginning with the date on which it was made (paragraph 6 of Schedule 3). The supervisor can apply for an extension, or further extensions, for any period subject to the order not running for more than three years in total beyond the original date. The one-year time limit is intended to ensure that after a reasonable period the effectiveness of the order and the circumstances of the child are reviewed and a decision taken about further steps, if any, with the child, parents and others concerned being given the opportunity to participate in further proceedings if necessary.

9.70 A supervision order is brought to an end by the court discharging the order, the making of a care order with respect to the child, the child reaching the age of 18 (Article 179) or if a court takes action under section 25(1)(a) or (b) of the Child Abduction and Custody Act 1985 which provides for the recognition and enforcement of foreign custody orders. The making of a supervision order automatically terminates any earlier care order or supervision order which would otherwise continue in force (paragraph 9 of Schedule 3). An interim supervision order may accompany a residence order in the circumstances described in Article 57(3).

Discharge of care orders and discharge and variation of supervision orders

9.71 Application for discharge of a care order may be made by any person having parental responsibility for the child, the child or a Trust (Article 58(1)). The court can deal with an application for discharge of a care order by substituting a supervision order without having to re-establish the threshold criteria in Article 50(2) (Article 58(5)). It needs only to have regard to the welfare principles and checklist in Article 3. The previous findings of fact in relation to the significant harm conditions will be treated as accepted findings in the new application to discharge the care order. The court's concern will focus on what, if any, alternative

CHILDREN ORDER

provisions can be made to safeguard and promote the welfare of the child.

9.72 If a Trust is seeking a care order in substitution for a supervision order, there is no similar provision to that under Article 58(5) discussed above. The Trust must satisfy the relevant criteria after a full hearing under Article 50(2). This is so even though the application will most likely arise from non-compliance with the terms of the original supervision order. Any care order then made will automatically discharge the existing supervision order (Article 179(3)).

9.73 Application for discharge or variation of a supervision order may be made by any person who has parental responsibility for the child, the child itself or the supervisor (Article 58(2)). This includes variation of a requirement imposed under the order in accordance with Schedule 3 and in such a case a person on whom the requirement is imposed may also apply for its variation. A court has power to make an Article 8 order whether or not it varies or discharges the supervision order.

9.74 A care order is automatically discharged by the making of a residence order (Article 179(1)). This route extends opportunities to bring a care order to an end to the following persons not having parental responsibility: Trust foster parents (if they satisfy the conditions in Article 9(3)), an unmarried father (Article 10(4)(a)), any person with whom the child has lived for at least three years (Article 10(5)(b)), any person who has the consent of a Trust to apply for a residence order (Article 10(5)(c)(ii)) and any person who succeeds in an application for leave to bring an application (Article 10(9)). When considering an application for leave, the court has to have regard, **inter alia**, to the Trust's plans for the child's future and the wishes and feelings of the child's parents. A person in whose favour a residence order is made, and who thereby acquires parental responsibility if he does not already have it, is able to apply for discharge or variation of a supervision order under Article 58(2)(a).

9.75 **Trusts are required by the Review of Children's Cases Regulations made under Article 45(2) to consider at least at every statutory review of a case of a child in Trust care whether to apply for discharge of the care order.** As part of each review the child has to be informed (according to his age

and level of understanding) of steps he may take, which include applying for discharge of the order, applying for a contact order or variation of an existing contact order or for leave to apply for a residence order (Article 10(8)). A Trust, in suitable cases, should also work towards bringing a care order to an end through rehabilitation of the child under Article 27(7). The Trust should prepare for his rehabilitation by advising, assisting and befriending the child under Article 35 and, if appropriate, by encouraging increased contact with the person or persons concerned (applying if necessary for variation of a contact order made under Article 53). The court does not have power to postpone discharge of a care order to allow for a gradual return of the child to his family over a period of time. However it can encourage the process of rehabilitation by varying the contact provisions consistent with a plan for return. It can also make a residence order with appropriate directions and conditions under Article 11(7) coupled with a supervision order.

9.76 The supervisor of a child under a supervision order must consider whether or not to apply for the order to be varied or discharged where it is not wholly complied with or he considers that the order may no longer be necessary. Cases of non-compliance can include cases where a child of sufficient understanding refuses consent to a medical or psychiatric examination (or treatment) required by the order. The supervisor should also review the need for, and reasonableness of, any directions he has given to the child or responsible person under the order, the arrangements made for carrying them out, and whether it would be in the interests of the child to change these. In considering whether to make application to the court, he should consider how the court would be likely to view the application using the checklist in Article 3(3).

9.77 The Children Order places a time limit on repeat applications (Article 179(15) and (16)). Where an application for discharge of a care order or supervision order or to substitute a supervision order for a care order has been disposed of, no further application of this kind may be made within six months without leave of the court. This does not apply to interim orders or applications to vary a supervision order.

Appeals against care and supervision orders

9.78 Rules of court provide that any one who had party status in the

original proceedings may appeal against the making of a care or supervision order (including an interim order) or of an order varying or discharging such an order, or against the court's refusal to make such an order. Trusts, like any other party, have full rights of appeal. Decisions by a court of summary jurisdiction are appealable to the county court and decisions by county courts are appealable to the High Court (Article 166(1)-(3)). Appeals against decisions of the High Court in care and supervision proceedings will go to the Court of Appeal (section 35 of the Judicature (Northern Ireland) Act 1978).

9.79 The Children Order sets out the court's order-making powers pending an appeal in specific circumstances in care or supervision proceedings (Article 59). The circumstances are where there is already some background of compulsory intervention in the child's upbringing. The court can exercise these powers when an intention to appeal is notified or when an appeal can be made but is still being considered. The basic approach is to maintain the **status quo** in order to provide continued protection for the child.

9.80 Thus, where the court dismisses an application for a care order and the child is at that time subject to an interim care order, the court may make a care order pending the appeal (Article 59(1)). If it dismisses an application for a care order or an application for a supervision order and the child is at that time subject to an interim supervision order, the court may make a supervision order pending the appeal (Article 59(2)). In each case the court can include directions in the order on any matter to do with the child's welfare that it considers appropriate. Where the court agrees to discharge a care or supervision order it may order that, pending the appeal, the decision is not to have effect, or that the order should remain in force subject to any directions it makes (Article 59(3)).

9.81 The court may determine the length of an order pending appeal but it cannot exceed the appeal period. Where an appeal is actually lodged this means the period between the decision and the final determination of the appeal. In other cases it means the period during which an appeal can be lodged (Article 59(4) and (6)).

9.82 An appeal can be made against a court's decision to make or

refuse to make an order pending appeal. The appellate court may then make the order if it thinks fit. It also has power to extend the duration of any order pending appeal made by a lower court but not beyond the appeal period as defined in Article 59(6). Furthermore, if the court makes a residence order in care or supervision proceedings, it can postpone the coming into effect of the order or impose temporary requirements pending an appeal.

9.83 Continuation of the proceedings may itself be unsettling for the child; the court must continue to have regard to the presumption against making an order in Article 3(5) and will need persuading that a pending-appeal order is required. The court's timetable for the case will need extending to provide for the appeal and should reflect the need to bring the proceedings to a conclusion as quickly as possible.

CHILDREN ORDER

CHAPTER 10: INTERIM CARE AND SUPERVISION ORDERS

10.1   Where, on an application for a care or supervision order, the proceedings are adjourned, or where the court in any proceedings gives a direction under Article 56(1) for a Trust to investigate the child's circumstances, the court may make an interim care or supervision order. The court has to be satisfied, whether the making of an interim order is contested or not, that there are **reasonable grounds for believing** that the child's circumstances fulfil the criteria for a full care or supervision order in Article 50(2).

10.2   This test is not the same as for a full order which requires proof that the child is suffering or likely to suffer significant harm. It would not be realistic to require proof of the condition at the interim stage when the guardian *ad litem's* final report will probably not have been received and all evidence heard. The child's version of events may form an integral part of "reasonable grounds for believing" as could, for example, medical evidence that certain symptoms were consistent with abuse. After further assessment this may be rejected at the full hearing. Court findings of fact leading to the making of interim orders should therefore not be binding on the court at the final hearing, and should not be regarded as prejudicial to any of the parties to the proceedings. As when making full orders, the court must also have regard to the child welfare principles and checklist in Article 3(1) and (3), and to the presumption against making an order in Article 3(5).

10.3   Interim care and supervision orders are similar to full care and supervision orders, except that the court determines the duration of the interim order and may give directions to the Trust as to medical or psychiatric examination of the child or other assessment. **These orders represent substantial, if temporary, intervention in the care and upbringing of the child, and should not be regarded as routine parts of an application for a full care or supervision order.** The interim supervision order may be an effective means of achieving a degree of control short of acquisition of parental responsibility and the power to remove the child from home, both of which are conferred on the holder of an interim care order. It may be useful for attaining a particular objective, for example that a child attends a local health centre for routine health checks.

10.4 An interim care order or interim supervision order will usually be the only way that protection can continue to be afforded to a child after expiry of an emergency protection order or a period of police protection, if such protection is required while enquiries are continuing. Where there continue to be indications that emergency action is warranted, the child's welfare should be the first consideration. The Trust should consider carefully, if an interim care order is made, whether the child could be allowed to live with his family.

10.5 The criteria for interim orders are intended to prevent "rubber-stamping" of unopposed applications. **The consequences of the repeated use of interim care orders can be so potentially serious for the child and those with parental responsibility for the child that such a step should always be fully examined.** The parents and others concerned should never be encouraged to consent to an interim order just to avoid the trauma of a court hearing. The less adversarial procedures for court hearings, the role of the directions appointment and advance disclosure, are intended to remove as much trauma as possible without loss of effectiveness. Nor will parental agreement be sufficient to satisfy the presumption of no order in Article 3(5).

10.6 The court is able to make an Article 8 order as an interim measure, but if it makes a residence order it must also make an interim supervision order unless satisfied that the child's welfare will be satisfactorily safeguarded without one (Articles 11(3) and 57(3)). A residence order made in these or any other circumstances gives the person with whom the child would live parental responsibility for the child while the order is in force. It may contain directions about how it is to be carried into effect, impose conditions which must be complied with, and be made to have effect for a specified period - which could be until the original care or supervision application is decided (Article 11(7)). Questions of contact between the child and the parents or other persons, the child's education and other matters to do with his welfare during this period, could be dealt with under these powers or by way of other Article 8 orders (contact orders, specific issue orders and prohibited steps orders). The court would not have the power to make a residence or contact order in favour of a Trust because of the restriction contained in Article 9(2).

10.7 Where a suitable relative or friend is prepared to look after the child and is likely to be able to meet his needs at least for a trial period, the residence order - supported where necessary by an interim supervision order - offers an attractive alternative to the interim care order. The Trust should always weigh carefully the pros and cons of such an arrangement. While there might be some danger in an arrangement which did not give control of the placement to the Trust, a temporary residence order might obviate the need for a full care order later if the interim arrangement proved an effective way of promoting the child's welfare. The Trust should ensure that support services provided under Part IV of the Children Order are made available to help the person caring for the child under a short-term residence order to meet the child's needs while the order is in force.

10.8 The court has specific power to give directions on medical or psychiatric examination or other assessment of the child when making an interim care or interim supervision order or at any time while an order is in force (Article 57(6) - see paragraphs 10.14-10.18). However, care proceedings should not be used simply to obtain an examination or assessment of the child. If the applicant's main concern at this stage is to secure such an examination or assessment and the parents cannot be persuaded to co-operate on a voluntary basis, a child assessment order should be sufficient. If the Trust believes an interim order is likely to be necessary, even though the child does not need to be removed, an interim supervision order is to be preferred. Medical and other assessment directions may be necessary where a child assessment order reveals only a partial picture of harm or failure to thrive, the Trust's concerns are not dispelled and further investigation is called for. Other directions provided for in Schedule 3 to the Children Order relating to supervision orders would be at the supervisor's discretion.

Duration of interim orders

10.9 An interim care or supervision order may be made for such period as the court orders but may not last longer than eight weeks in the case of an initial order or "the relevant period" in the case of a second or subsequent order (Article 57(4)). The relevant period is four weeks, or eight weeks from the date of the first order if that is longer. Thus, if the first order was made

for two weeks, the second order could be made for six weeks. If the first two orders were made respectively for one and two weeks, the third order could be made for five weeks (the eight-week threshold does not apply in reverse, ie where the first order is made for five weeks say, the second order does not have to be limited to three weeks: the four week limit takes over).

10.10   When deciding how long an interim order should last the court must consider whether any party who was, or might have been, opposed to the making of the order was in a position to fully argue his case against the order (Article 57(10)). Where, for example, a parent has not had sufficient time to instruct a lawyer in the proceedings, the court may decide to make a short interim order so that the parent can be properly represented at an early next hearing.

10.11   There is no limit in principle to the number of interim orders which the court can make, provided they are made before the expiry of the relevant period. Before making a further interim order the court must satisfy itself that the criteria in Article 57(2) and Article 3(5) are still satisfied - not by going over the evidence again but by considering any change in the circumstances, any new evidence that may have come to light and any other relevant matter that may cast doubt on the benefit of a new order. An interim order ceases to have effect on disposal of the application for a care or supervision order.

10.12   If, in family proceedings, a court orders an investigation by a Trust under Article 56(1), the court may make an interim care or supervision order to safeguard the welfare of the child. In such a case, the order will cease to have effect at the end of the period fixed by the court (if any) for the Trust to report to it. The maximum period is eight weeks (Article 56(4)). The Trust may decide within that period to commence to obtain a care or supervision order. If an application is made and the proceedings on that application are adjourned, an interim order made then would be the second order and subject to the time limit for second and subsequent orders described above.

10.13   The intention is that a flexible initial time limit, backed by timetabling and reviews of progress, will expedite the final hearing on applications for care or supervision orders. The court, when deciding the timetabling of a case, will nevertheless

need satisfying on the need for a long interim order and it would not be expected that four week applications for subsequent orders would be made. Although there is no limit to the number of interim orders that can be made under the Children Order, a balance will have to be struck between allowing sufficient time for inquiries, reports and statements, and risking allowing the child to continue in interim care or supervision for so long that the balance of advantage is distorted in favour of continued intervention. Subject to that, the emphasis should be very firmly on pressing on to a final hearing as quickly as possible (unless, of course, the matter can be resolved by negotiation without further compulsory intervention out of court). The guardian *ad litem* will have a key role in advising the court on interim orders - whether one should be made and if so which, for how long, whether directions are required on examinations and assessment, and on contact where an interim care order is made. The applicant should make his views known on these matters to the guardian *ad litem*, who will also want to establish the views of other parties, including the child.

Directions on examination and assessment when an interim order is made

10.14 The Children Order gives the court a power when making an interim care order or interim supervision order to give any directions it considers appropriate about medical or psychiatric examination or other assessment of the child (Article 57(6)). The court can prohibit examination or assessment altogether or make this subject to its specific approval (Article 57(7)). Directions can be given when the order is made or at any other time while it is in force. They are not appealable but may be varied on an application made in accordance with rules of court by any party who was a party to the proceedings in which the directions were given. Article 57(6) makes clear that if the child is of sufficient understanding he may refuse to submit to the examination or assessment.

10.15 The court has similar directions powers in support of the child assessment order (Article 62(6)(b)) and emergency protection order (Article 63(6)(b)). The court does not, however, have power to give directions when making a full care order (decisions on examinations and assessment fall within the Trust's

parental responsibility, subject to the consent of a child of sufficient understanding) and its powers are more limited when a full supervision order is made. Paragraphs 4 and 5 of Schedule 3 to the Children Order on psychiatric and medical examinations and treatment under a supervision order do not apply when an interim supervision order is made (Article 57(9)); such matters have to be dealt with by court directions (though the court's power does not extend to treatment). Children should not be subjected to repeated medical examinations solely for evidential purposes, and where examination and interview is necessary they should be carried out in a suitable and sensitive environment with appropriately trained staff available. Local inter-agency arrangements should aim to establish a pool of health and other professionally trained experts who may be called on to participate in a wide-ranging programme of multi-disciplinary assessments and examinations. Considerations of the gender, ethnic and cultural identity of the child concerned will play a part in determining the programme of assessment and the manner in which it is undertaken.

10.16　An assessment, and maybe an examination, of the child will often be necessary as evidence showing whether the child is suffering, or is likely to suffer, significant harm - the first threshold condition for a full care or supervision order. In some cases this may have been carried out before the care or supervision proceedings, perhaps by agreement with the parents or under a child assessment order. In other cases the applicant should consider whether satisfactory arrangements can be made without the need for an interim order and court directions. The applicant should try to discuss his proposals with the parents, the child (if of sufficient understanding) and the guardian *ad litem* before the adjourned hearing. The aim should be to secure the agreement of all concerned to a single programme of examination or assessment, which could if necessary be observed by, or conducted jointly with, a medical practitioner nominated by the child's parents. Parental agreement must always be balanced by the need to safeguard and protect the welfare of a child who may be at risk and this will mean ensuring that the assessment is carried out by those properly trained to do so. If the parents are co-operative, satisfactory arrangements can be made by agreement, and there is no immediate risk to the child's welfare, it may be unnecessary to seek an interim order and directions. If there are

any doubts or where any aspect of the assessment is likely to prove contentious - for example, a possibility that if the examination found abuse the parents would want a second opinion requiring further examination of the child - the better course in the child's interests may be to seek an interim supervision order and court control by directions. The court will expect to be advised on these matters by the guardian *ad litem*, who will need to elicit the child's views and the positions of the applicant and the parents. In the last resort and where there is a conflict of views between the parties (the parents, the applicant and the guardian *ad litem*) the court must determine the type of assessment to be carried out and by whom based on the nature of the concern and what is in the best interests of the child.

10.17 Court directions on examinations or assessment do not override the right of the child who is of sufficient understanding to make an informed decision to refuse to submit to an examination or assessment. Examination or assessment without consent may be held in law to be an assault. For consent to be valid the person giving consent must be aware of what he is consenting to (and the possible consequences) and be freely given. A child of 16 is presumed in law to be capable of giving or withholding consent unless there is some mental incapacity to giving consent. Depending on their age and understanding, younger children may also be regarded by a doctor as capable of giving consent to examination or assessment. In all such cases it is the child's consent that is relevant, not that given by anyone else. Article 57(6) (and the similar provisions in Articles 62 and 63) restate the position of the child of sufficient understanding in order to make clear beyond doubt that the child's consent is required even where the court makes directions. For younger children who are not regarded by a doctor as capable of giving consent, consent would normally have to be obtained from parents. If an interim care order were made, the necessary parental responsibility would be acquired by the Trust, although the Trust may have to use powers to restrict parents' exercise of parental responsibility. In other cases, for example where a specific issue arises and a private law Article 8 order is sought, court directions could override the parents' ability to refuse consent.

10.18 The court will probably want to know, when considering giving

directions on examination or assessment for the older child, whether the child is of sufficient age and understanding to give or withhold consent; if so, how the child intends to respond; if there is any possibility of the child being put under pressure to refuse consent; and whether, as a result, the proposed order and directions are likely to be effective. The court will usually look to the guardian *ad litem* for advice on these matters. All have a duty to ensure that where the child is of sufficient age and understanding that his views are made known. Where a child's first language is not English, or where, because of a child's physical disability, communication methods other than speech and written language are necessary, expert assistance will be required to meet this responsibility. For a mentally handicapped child of sufficient age such assistance will be necessary to determine the child's capacity to understand. Directions by the court will not absolve the doctor or other person conducting the examination or assessment from his responsibility to be satisfied that a child of sufficient age and understanding consents. He should not proceed if such consent is withheld. He should arrange for the facts of the matter to be reported to the court which gave the directions as soon as possible, usually via the guardian *ad litem*, so that the court may reconsider the direction. The interim order can be varied only on application by one of the parties.

Effects of, and responsibilities arising from, interim orders

10.19 By virtue of Article 49(1) interim orders have the same effect and give the same responsibilities to Trusts as full orders, save for the differences noted in paragraph 10.3, namely that the court determines the length of the order and may give directions for examination and assessment. In particular, the Trust acquires parental responsibility for the child for as long as the interim care order is in force. The provisions on contact with the child also apply in interim care cases (Article 53). Interim supervision orders do not confer parental responsibility on the Trust and therefore contact with the child may only be controlled by an Article 8 contact order. Before making an Article 53 order, the court must consider the Trust's proposals for contact and may invite the other parties to the proceedings to comment on them; and it may make an order under Article 53 whether or not an application is made (see Chapter 12). The

Trust's responsibilities following the making of an interim care order include reviewing the child's case in accordance with the regulations made under Article 45(1) and the duty to comply with Article 27 and the relevant regulations when placing the child. In particular, this means that the placement with a parent, relative, friend or person connected with the child should be considered as a first option unless this would not be reasonably practicable or consistent with the child's welfare (Article 27(7)). When reviewing the case the Trust must consider whether to apply for discharge of the order and to inform the child of steps he may take under the Children Order. The temporary nature of the interim order should be allowed for in the exercise of these responsibilities, but it is not a reason for not taking them seriously.

10.20 It may very exceptionally arise that an authorised person obtains an interim care order without having been able to consult the Trust as required by Article 50(7) - perhaps after emergency action when it is not immediately clear in which area the child is ordinarily resident. In these circumstances the authorised person may keep the child in his care but the authorised person and the designated Trust should arrange for the latter to take over care of the child as soon as possible. The authorised person would not have parental responsibility (a full or interim care order confers parental responsibility only on the designated Trust specified in the order) but would have actual care of the child and authority to do what is reasonable for safeguarding or promoting the child's welfare (Article 6(5)). If it were necessary for the child to be accommodated overnight before the designated Trust could take over his care, it could seek help from the authorised person or one of the bodies listed in Article 46(3). Article 46(4) allows reimbursement of reasonable expenses incurred by another Trust in providing assistance.

CHILDREN ORDER

CHAPTER 11 : WARDSHIP AND THE INHERENT JURISDICTION OF THE HIGH COURT

11.1 The impact of the Children Order on the inherent jurisdiction of the High Court will be considerable. By incorporating many of the beneficial aspects of wardship, such as the "open door" policy, and a flexible range of orders, the Order will substantially reduce the need to have recourse to the High Court. In addition, there is a specific prohibition against using the inherent jurisdiction in general, and wardship in particular, as an alternative to public law orders. Without this prohibition, the threshold criteria which have been carefully designed as the minimum circumstances justifying State intervention would be undermined, as too would any directions attached to these orders (such as to their duration or other effects). Where a wardship court thinks that a care or supervision order may be needed, it may direct a Trust to investigate the child's circumstances with a view to the Trust making an application under Article 50 and to make an interim care or supervision order pending the outcome of the Trust's decision. These are the same powers that are available to any court in family proceedings. Similarly, since proceedings under the inherent jurisdiction are family proceedings, it is open to the court to make an Article 8 order.

11.2 The Children Order also affects the relationship between wardship and Trust care. Under the old law it was possible for a child in compulsory care also to be a ward of court. Wardship in these circumstances could only be invoked with the Trust's agreement. While the child was a ward of court, the Trust's powers were uncertain because, in wardship, the court is said to be the child's guardian. The Trust's powers were restricted by the rule which required major decisions in the child's life to be referred to the court. In future, where a child is in care, this division of responsibility should not occur. The Trust has parental responsibility for the child and should be able to take whatever decisions are necessary. The Children Order therefore makes wardship and care incompatible. If a ward of court is committed to care the wardship ceases to have effect (Article 179(4)). While a child is in care he cannot be made a ward of court (Article 173(1) and section 26 of the Judicature (Northern Ireland) Act 1978 as amended by paragraph 90 of Schedule 9 to the Children Order).

11.3 The restrictions imposed by the Children Order do not prevent the High Court from exercising its inherent jurisdiction to decide a specific question in relation to a child in care. The inherent jurisdiction remains available as a remedy of last resort where a Trust seeks the resolution of a specific issue concerning the future of a child in its care. But there are restrictions: the first is that a Trust must have the High Court's leave to apply for the exercise of its inherent jurisdiction (Article 173(2)). Leave may only be granted where the court is satisfied that the Trust could not achieve the desired result through the making of any order other than one under the inherent jurisdiction (Article 173(3)(a)). Where there are statutory remedies within the Children Order, the Trust will be expected to pursue those. In particular, where a child is not in care, the Trust will rarely be granted leave since it could otherwise obtain a specific issue or prohibited steps order under Article 8. An exception might be where the Trust seeks to restrain publicity about the child. Second, even where there is no other statutory remedy within the Children Order, there must be reasonable cause to believe that the child is likely to suffer significant harm if the inherent jurisdiction is not exercised (Article 173(3)(b)).

11.4 Since a Trust will have parental responsibility for children in its care it should make decisions itself in consultation with the parents as appropriate and after taking the child's views into account. Nevertheless there may be occasions where recourse to the High Court is appropriate as the decisions to be taken are highly contentious, and/or fall far outside the normal scope of decision-making for children in care. For example the inherent jurisdiction might be invoked to overcome an anorexic child in care to consent to medical treatment. Other examples of medical treatment where leave might be given include sterilisation and contested cases involving emergency treatment of a child in care. Other less extreme situations may also merit High Court intervention, for example, to restrain harmful publicity about the child. In such cases when the inherent jurisdiction is the only means of obtaining the remedy, it may not be too difficult to satisfy the leave criteria.

11.5 The Children Order further prevents the High Court from exercising its inherent jurisdiction "for the purposes of conferring on any Trust power to determine any question which has arisen, or which may arise in connection with any aspect of

parental responsibility". Thus, in making an order under its inherent jurisdiction, the court cannot confer on a Trust any degree of parental responsibility it does not already have (Article 173(1)).

11.6   On commencement of Part V of the Children Order all wards of court committed into the care of the Department of Health and Social Services or a Trust (other than those where proceedings are regarded as "pending"), cease to be wards (paragraph 13(1) of Schedule 8). Similarly, those children who are in care and subsequently made wards of court and who thereafter continued to be in care, cease to be wards from the commencement of Part V of the Children Order (paragraph 13(2) of Schedule 8). In each of the above mentioned circumstances the child concerned remains in care under what is deemed to be a care order made under Article 50 of the Children Order. However, any directions made prior to commencement of the Children Order will effectively become "free-standing" and remain in force until varied or discharged by the court (paragraph 12(4) of Schedule 8). Such directions attach themselves to the deemed care order. As soon after commencement as is reasonably practicable Trusts will wish to seek a discharge or variation of these directions where they appear to unduly fetter Trusts' exercise of their parental responsibility and hamper effective management of a child in their care. They will also need to consider whether to seek the conversion of care orders triggered by the transitional provisions into other orders. The High Court's intention in making the original order will be one of the factors a Trust should take into account. For example, where a child, prior to commencement of the Children Order, was in the care and control of the Department or a Trust, by virtue of the High Court's inherent jurisdiction but placed with the child's own family, a residence order coupled with a supervision order might provide a more appropriate remedy.

11.7   Special arrangements will apply with respect to wards of court who have been placed or allowed to remain in the care of the Department or a Trust in wardship under an interim order and who are still in care one year after the commencement of paragraph 1(2) of Schedule 8 to the Children Order (paragraph 12(1) of Schedule 8). These cases will no longer be regarded as "pending proceedings" and any interim order made in these wardship proceedings will be treated as if a final order had been

CHILDREN ORDER

made and, by virtue of paragraph 12(2) of Schedule 8, will be deemed to be a care order made under Article 50 and the wardship will cease.

CHILDREN ORDER

CHAPTER 12: CONTACT WITH CHILDREN IN CARE

12.1   Provisions concerning contact with children in care are separate from the contact provisions in Part III of the Children Order regulating visiting or staying in the private law. If a child is in the care of a Trust, no court can make an Article 8 contact order (Article 9(1)). If there is a contact order under Article 8 in existence it is automatically discharged on the making of a care order (Article 179(2)).

12.2   Contact with children who are the subject of care orders is governed by Article 53. It establishes that a Trust must allow a child reasonable contact with his parents and certain other people, unless directed otherwise by a court order, or the Trust temporarily suspends contact in urgent circumstances. It requires the court to consider contact arrangements before making a care order and gives it wide powers to deal with problems. The underlying principle is that the Trust, child and other persons concerned should as far as possible agree reasonable arrangements before the care order is made, but should be able to seek the court's assistance if agreement cannot be reached or the Trust wants to deny contact to a person who is otherwise entitled to it under the Children Order. Every effort should be made to enter into constructive agreements on contact, mindful of the integrity and security of the placement. However, it should be recognised that there will be cases where contact will be detrimental to the child's welfare. This possibility should be considered at the pre-court proceedings stage, when plans for contact are being drawn up. Applications for orders prohibiting contact are discussed at paragraph 12.7 below.

12.3   The presumption that contact is allowed for certain named people, and the pro-active role given to the court reflect the importance of this subject. Regular contact with parents, relatives and friends will usually be an important part of the child's upbringing in his new environment and is essential to successful rehabilitation. Lack of contact can, over a period, have vital consequences for the rights of parents and children; it can be a major factor in deciding whether to discharge a care order or to dispense with parental agreement to adoption. This is too important to be regarded as simply a matter of management within the sole control of a Trust.

12.4 Article 53(1) requires a Trust to allow a child reasonable contact with his parents, any guardian, and any person having the benefit of a residence order or care of the child under wardship immediately before the care order was made (on the making of which the residence order or wardship lapses). The parent includes an unmarried father. Subject to any court order, it is for a Trust to decide what is reasonable contact in the circumstances. The degree of contact should not necessarily remain static; a Trust may plan for the frequency or duration of contact to increase or decrease over time. Again this should be specified in the plan which is prepared and submitted to the court prior to the making of an order. Where possible, the plan should have been discussed with the child and his parents; any disagreements can be resolved by the court making an order as to the degree of contact.

12.5 There are a number of ways in which a Trust's proposals for contact may be scrutinised or challenged:

(a) the court, before making a care order, must consider the arrangements made or proposed by a Trust and ask parents to the proceedings to comment on them (Article 53(11)). The guardian *ad litem* is also likely to comment on the arrangements with the child's interests in mind;

(b) any person to whom the Children Order's presumption of reasonable contact applies, or any other person who has obtained the leave of the court, can apply for an order about contact at any time if they are dissatisfied with the arrangements made or proposed for contact with the child;

(c) the child can do the same, and can also apply for his contact with another person to be reduced, suspended or terminated;

(d) the court, if it is satisfied that it should do so under Article 3(5), can make any order about contact that it considers appropriate either in response to an application or on its own initiative, and can impose any conditions it considers appropriate. The conditions can be as specific as the court judges necessary, for example, that contact is supervised or takes place at a particular time or place, or is reviewed at prescribed intervals.

CHILDREN ORDER

12.6 A Trust has the same powers as the child to apply for a court order, and can also refuse contact that would otherwise be required by virtue of the statutory entitlement or a court order for a limited period without reference to the court. It must be satisfied that this is necessary in order to safeguard or promote the child's welfare, and the refusal must be decided upon as a matter of urgency and not last for more than seven days (Article 53(6)). The person concerned or the child may apply to the court for an order in response to such a decision. If a Trust considers it necessary to refuse contact for a longer period it must apply for an order under Article 53(4), whereupon under rules of court the person concerned and the child may contest the application. The Trust, child or person named in the order may apply at any time for an order to be varied or discharged; and any party to the proceedings (including the Trust) can appeal against the making of, or refusal to make, an order.

12.7 Action to set aside contact under Article 53(6) is a serious step which should not be undertaken lightly. That said, the Trust should not hesitate to use this power if contact with a particular person or persons proves harmful or potentially harmful to the child's welfare. There must however be some sudden new circumstance or rapid deterioration in relations with the child to justify deciding the refusal as a matter of urgency. It must not be a response to cumulative problems which can be seen developing over a period of time. In such cases the proper course for a Trust is to try to negotiate a reduction or even termination of contact and, if that does not succeed, to apply for an order under either Article 53(2) or (4) (and, if necessary, conditions under Article 53(7)) or, if an order already exists, for variation or discharge under Article 53(9). Regulation 3 of the Contact with Children Regulations outlines the actions which a Trust is required to take before it can depart from the terms of a court order on contact. If agreement cannot be reached, and the conditions outlined in Article 53(6) (enabling a Trust to temporarily suspend contact in order to safeguard the child's welfare - see paragraph 12.6 above) do not apply, a Trust will have to consider applying to the court for an order restricting contact.

12.8 Article 53(6) applies only to situations where a Trust wishes to refuse contact to a person to whom the presumption of reasonable contact under Article 53(1) applies, or who is the beneficiary of an order. However, there may also be occasions or

CHILDREN ORDER

circumstances where it is important to refuse contact to a person who is not entitled to contact, but has nevertheless been having contact with the child. In such cases it may be helpful to apply the principle outlined in Article 53(6) - that contact should only be denied in order to safeguard or promote the child's welfare. A Trust can invoke its care management duties in such cases; contact should be refused immediately in urgent circumstances, but in general, and to ensure consistency in the refusal of contact, the requirements of Article 53(6) should be satisfied. In non-urgent cases, a Trust should give the person concerned notice of its intention to end contact between the person and the child. This should be discussed with the child if he is of sufficient age and understanding. The person concerned should be provided with details of the representations procedure which Trusts are obliged to set up under Article 45, and informed of his right to apply to the court for leave to make an application for an order under Article 53(3). If agreement cannot be reached, particularly if the person had previously enjoyed contact with the child, the Trust should apply for an order as quickly as possible or encourage the person concerned to do so, so that the impact of refusal of contact on the child can be tested by the court.

12.9 Repeat applications for contact orders under Article 53 are controlled by Article 179(17). If an application for an order has been refused, the person concerned may not re-apply for the same order in respect of the same child within six months without court leave. This prohibition applies to all proceedings under Article 53 including applications to vary or discharge existing orders. The court would expect to hear of a change in circumstances sufficient to justify a departure from this rule, which is designed to discourage frequent rehearings of the same case. A Trust is not exempt from this restriction; however, it will be expected to carry out good child care practice, seeking the leave of the court to vary or discharge a contact order as appropriate. The court also has a more general power under Article 179(14) to prevent applications being made without the leave of the court. This provision may be used to prevent a vexatious litigant from making repeated applications for contact with little chance of success.

12.10 Certain other provisions in the Children Order bear on the question of contact. A Trust has a general duty to promote contact between the child and his parents, others who have

parental responsibility and relatives, friends and others (Article 29). The Trust must take reasonable steps to keep certain of these people informed of the child's whereabouts, unless it has reasonable cause for believing that giving that information would be prejudicial to the child's welfare. Information must also be given where another Trust takes over the provision of accommodation. Information about the child may only be withheld where it is essential to the welfare of the child, and where the child is in the care of the Trust by virtue of an order under Article 50. If the child is being looked after on a voluntary basis, the provisions of Article 29(4) do not apply and a Trust is not entitled to withhold information. Where a Trust provides accommodation, including the placing of the child with a foster parent it must try to ensure that the accommodation is near the child's home, so that contact is facilitated.

12.11 A Trust may promote contact by helping with the costs incurred in making visits (Article 30). This help may be given to the parent (or other person who is entitled to contact with the child) or to the child. The general duty of a Trust to promote contact between a child and his parents should be borne in mind when determining whether such assistance should be provided. Thus a Trust should ensure that the parents and child are aware that such assistance is available when plans for contact are being discussed.

12.12 **Children with special needs, or who have difficulty in communicating, may need extra Trust support to help them to maintain contact when placed at a distance from their home area.** Contact includes communication by letter and telephone, and some children may need special provisions to facilitate this type of contact. Particular consideration must also be given to the needs of children for whom their first language (or that of their parent) is not English. Again, plans for contact should include the arrangements which a Trust proposes to make in respect of the particular needs of the child in question.

CHILDREN ORDER

CHAPTER 13: EDUCATION SUPERVISION ORDERS

13.1   Under the Children Order, it will no longer be possible for a child to be taken into care on purely educational grounds. Article 55 of the Children Order creates a new type of order aimed solely at school attendance cases: the education supervision order.

13.2   Under Article 55 a court may make an education supervision order on the application of an education and library board if it is satisfied that the child concerned is of compulsory school age and is not being properly educated. The education supervision order replaces previous legislation under which children could be taken into care as a consequence of truancy, and offers one means of dealing with non-attendance at school when other arrangements have failed. Provision for action against parents under the Education and Libraries (Northern Ireland) Order 1986 still applies.

13.3   The specific grounds in Schedule 13 to the Education and Libraries (Northern Ireland) Order 1986 which allowed for a training school order, fit person order or supervision order to be sought if the child was not receiving proper education and was deemed to be in need of care, protection and control are repealed. The Children Order also amends Schedule 13 to the 1986 Order so that courts may no longer direct that care proceedings be taken with regard to a child whose parents have been prosecuted under paragraph 4 of that Schedule. The intention of education supervision orders is to ensure that a child who is subject to such an order receives efficient full-time education suited to his age, ability, aptitude and any special educational needs, and that sufficient support, advice and guidance are provided to the parents and the child.

Scope of legislation

13.4   Article 55(2) of the Children Order provides for an education supervision order to be made only if the court is satisfied that a child of compulsory school age is not being properly educated ie the child is not receiving full-time education suitable to his age, ability and aptitude and any special educational needs he may have (Article 55(3)). Unless proved otherwise, this ground

is deemed to be satisfied if the child is the subject of a school attendance order which is not being complied with, or if the child is not attending regularly the school at which he is a registered pupil (Article 55(4)).

13.5 There is no power to make an education supervision order if a child is in care (Article 55(5)) but an order can be made in respect of a child under supervision or accommodated by or on behalf of a Trust. Trusts have an equal duty to that of parents to discharge their obligations in relation to children in their care ie to ensure that the child continues to receive full-time education suitable to his age, ability and aptitude and any special educational needs he may have.

13.6 In the event of continuing difficulties in relation to a child accommodated by or on behalf of a Trust, the Trust must consult the education and library board in order to ensure the child's continuing access to education. Where necessary, the education and library board can make an application for an education supervision order if the board and Trust agree that this is necessary.

Effect of education supervision order

13.7 An education supervision order places a child under the supervision of an education and library board which may then give directions for his proper education. Paragraph 2 of Schedule 4 provides that directions attached to the order apply to both the child and to the parents of the child. "Parent" has the same meaning as in the Education and Libraries (Northern Ireland) Order 1986, where parent is defined as including any person who is not a parent of the child but who has parental responsibility for him or a person who has care of the child (paragraph 1 of Schedule 4).

13.8 The education and library board designated in the education supervision order must be the board within whose area the child is living or will live, or the education and library board within whose area the school at which the child is a registered pupil is situated if that board and the board in whose area the child lives agree (Article 55(6)). If a family moves to another area during the currency of an education supervision order, the

education and library board designated in the order should notify the education and library board to whose area the child is moving and consider with that board whether to apply to the court for the discharge of the original order and the making of a new order in favour of the receiving board. This will normally be appropriate unless the original education and library board is the one in whose area the school attended by the child is situated and the child is not changing school.

13.9   Where a parent fails to cause a child to receive efficient full-time education suitable to his age, ability and aptitude and any special educational needs he may have, an education and library board may either institute proceedings under Article 45 of, and Schedule 13 to, the Education and Libraries (Northern Ireland) Order 1986, whereby the parent may be prosecuted, or apply for an education supervision order, whichever is most likely to be effective in the circumstances.

13.10   It is important to remember that education supervision order proceedings under Article 55 of, and Schedule 4 to, the Children Order are "family proceedings" as defined in Article 8(3) and (4) of the Children Order. This means that when a court is considering an application for an education supervision order, the child's welfare shall be the paramount consideration. In particular the court must have regard to the considerations listed in Article 3(3), and it may call for welfare reports and for a hearing to be adjourned for preparation of such reports. The court is required to have regard to the general principle that any delay in determining a question which relates to the upbringing of a child is likely to prejudice his welfare (Article 3(2)). In addition, the court should not make an order unless this would be better for the child than making no order at all (Article 3(5)). These principles apply when all applications for court orders are made under the Children Order.

13.11   There may be some situations where the education and library board may decide not to apply for an education supervision order because it is unlikely to be effective. Where, for example, parents would be hostile to such intervention, it may not be possible to undertake the structured programme of work that is necessary. Alternative strategies may need to be considered by education and library boards in these situations, for example, the use of proceedings under Article 45 of, and Schedule 13 to,

the Education and Libraries (Northern Ireland) Order 1986 or discussions with the Trust on possible courses of action.

13.12 An education supervision order could help where parents find it difficult to exercise a proper influence over their child, and where the child has developed a pattern of poor attendance. It would give the backing of the court to the supervising officer and could complement the efforts of the supervising officer to resolve the child's problems by working with the parents to bring them to accept their statutory education responsibilities.

Duty to consult

13.13 When proposing to seek an education supervision order, the education and library board is required by Article 55(7) of the Children Order to consult the Trust in whose area the child lives, or if the child is being provided with accommodation by or on behalf of a Trust, that Trust. The Trust may decide to provide support for the child and his family under Part IV of the Children Order or apply for a compulsory order under Part V. Delay can be detrimental to the child's education. Education and library boards and Trusts should agree time-scales for such consultation and make these public. The outcome should be confirmed in writing, and should indicate whether or not the Trust is involved with the family, if there are any known reasons why an education supervision order would not be considered appropriate and what support the Trust is currently offering or will be offering the child and the family. Where the Trust is already involved it may require the assistance of the education and library board, which is under a duty to comply with the request in accordance with Article 46 of the Children Order, provided the request is specific as to what action is required, is compatible with its own statutory or other duties and does not unduly prejudice the discharge of any of its functions.

Powers and responsibilities of the court

13.14 It will be open to the courts, when considering proceedings under Article 45 of, and Schedule 13 to, the Education and Libraries (Northern Ireland) Order 1986 to direct the education and library board to apply for an education supervision order. In

such circumstances, the education and library board will need to consult with the appropriate Trust to determine whether it is necessary to make an education supervision order in order to safeguard the child's welfare.

13.15 When the court directs the education and library board to apply for an education supervision order, the education and library board is required to determine whether there are any reasons why it would not be appropriate to make such an application. If the board intends not to follow the direction of the court, a report outlining its reasons should be presented to the court within eight weeks beginning with the date on which the direction was given (paragraph 6(2) and (3) of Schedule 13 to the Education and Libraries (Northern Ireland) Order 1986 as amended by the Children Order).

Preparation for an education supervision order

13.16 Before considering applying for an education supervision order, all reasonable efforts should have been made by all the parties to resolve a problem of poor attendance without the use of legal sanctions.

13.17 An education supervision order removes from parents rights of appeal against admissions decisions and certain rights to have the child educated in accordance with their wishes. Parents should be made fully aware of this before an order is sought. They should also be made aware of their legal duty to comply with directions made under the order, of the penalties to which they may be liable if they persistently fail to comply with directions (paragraph 8 of Schedule 4), and of their rights of appeal under Article 166 (see paragraph 13.29 below). The child and the family should be told that if the child persistently fails to comply with directions, then the law requires the Trust to investigate the circumstances (paragraph 9 of Schedule 4).

Conduct of an education supervisor

13.18 The duties required of the supervising officer are "to advise, assist, befriend and give directions to" the child and the parents.

The objective is to ensure that the child receives efficient full-time education suitable to his age, ability, aptitude and any special educational needs, and that the child benefits fully from the education received. The aim is to establish and strengthen parental responsibility, and to enable the parents to discharge their responsibility towards the child.

13.19 Article 50 of the Children Order provides for the making of care orders and supervision orders. Where it appears to the supervising officer that sufficient grounds exist for the making of a care order or a supervision order on a child who is subject to an education supervision order, then this matter should be discussed between the education and library board and the appropriate Trust. It may be that the Trust can help with the provision of services under Schedule 2 to the Children Order which would make court proceedings unnecessary.

Change of school

13.20 Under paragraph 3 of Schedule 4 to the Children Order, parents lose their right to have the child educated in accordance with their wishes while an education supervision order is in force. They no longer have the right to move their child to another school and have no right of appeal against admissions decisions. It may be, however, that a change of school could be of benefit to the child, and the supervising officer should be sensitive to such matters and ready to act on behalf of the child. The parents' temporary loss of rights in this matter need not prevent a change of educational provision should it be necessary. Nor should the loss of parents' rights prevent discussion with them about the arrangements for the education of their child.

The use of directions

13.21 Paragraph 2 of Schedule 4 empowers the supervising officer to give directions to the supervised child or the parent. The supervisor is duty bound to consider the wishes and feelings of the child and parents (paragraph 2(2) and (3) of Schedule 4) and to ensure that the directions are reasonable. Supervisors should keep in mind that it is a defence in the case of prosecution if

parents can show that directions are unreasonable (paragraph 8(2)(b) of Schedule 4).

13.22 Directions might include, for example, a requirement for the parents and the child to attend meetings with the supervisor or with teachers at the school to discuss the child's progress. They may need to cover such areas as medical treatment or examination, or assessment by an educational psychologist.

13.23 Directions should be confirmed in writing, and where a child is being given a direction the parents also need to be told of this in writing. Written confirmation could be given at the same time as the direction is explained to the parent or child.

13.24 If parents fail to comply with a reasonable direction, they need to be told in writing that under an education supervision order they are required to follow the directions of the supervising officer and that they may be guilty of an offence if they persistently fail to comply. Upon conviction, the parents will be liable to a fine not exceeding level 3 on the standard scale.

Compliance with directions

13.25 Where a parent or a child persistently fails to comply with a direction given under the order, the supervising officer should ensure that the appropriate Trust is informed. In such cases, the Trust must investigate the circumstances of the child and consider whether it is appropriate for it to take any action to secure the welfare of the child (paragraph 9 of Schedule 4). In doing so, it may need to seek the views of other support services, but it should not lose sight of the need to move quickly so as to bring about real improvement. If it is clear that improvements in attendance are not being achieved, the Trust has a duty to consider seeking a care order under Article 50 of the Children Order, following the criteria laid down in Article 3.

Ceasing or extending an education supervision order

13.26 An education supervision order will normally cease to be

effective after one year or when the child is no longer of compulsory school age (paragraph 5 of Schedule 4). However, the court may discharge the order before that time on the application of the child, the parents or the education and library board (paragraph 7(1) of Schedule 4).

13.27   The supervising officer may seek the discharge because the objectives of the order have been met before the completion of a full year. This may be because the child is in receipt of efficient full-time education and there is good reason to believe that the parents are able to ensure that this is likely to continue for the foreseeable future.

13.28   An education supervision order may be extended for up to three years if an application is made by the education and library board. An extension may be sought where the supervising officer feels it necessary to ensure the continuing progress of the child's education. An application for an extension can only be made within the last three months of the order and must be heard before it expires (paragraph 5(2) and (3) of Schedule 4). An order can be extended more than once but no single extension may exceed three years. In any case, the order ceases to have effect if a care order is made or the child ceases to be of compulsory school age (paragraph 5(6) of Schedule 4).

13.29   Under Article 166 of the Children Order, parents have a right of appeal against the making of an education supervision order. Depending on which court made the order any appeal would lie to the county court, the High Court or the Court of Appeal.

Effect where child is subject to other court orders

13.30   A child who is the subject of an education supervision order may also be the subject of a supervision order, a probation order or an order made under section 74(1)(c) of the Children and Young Persons Act (Northern Ireland) 1968 (power of juvenile court to make a supervision order on a finding of guilt).

13.31   There are similar aspects to the orders, but the education supervision order is specifically concerned with ensuring that the child receives an adequate education. There will be different supervising officers and it will be necessary for them to

co-ordinate their efforts and to develop a clear understanding of their respective roles. There may well be scope for co-operative work; it will be necessary to maintain good lines of communication and to ensure that the parents and the child are fully aware of the different roles of the supervising officers. Failure to comply with a direction under an education supervision order is to be disregarded if it would not have been reasonably practicable to comply with it without failing to comply with a direction given under another order (paragraph 4 of Schedule 4).

Duties of Trusts in relation to education and library boards and education supervision orders

13.32   A Trust may be required to investigate the circumstances of a child when an education supervision order is discharged, or where a child persistently fails to comply with the directions of the supervising officer (paragraphs 7(2) and 9(2) of Schedule 4). This may be indicative of a particular need or of potential harm necessitating assessment. If this is required, the Trust must consider whether it would be appropriate to provide services under Part IV of, and Schedule 2 to, the Children Order or to initiate proceedings under Article 50 of that Order.

CHILDREN ORDER

CHAPTER 14: EMERGENCY PROTECTION ORDERS

14.1   Part VI of the Children Order fundamentally recasts the law on protecting children at risk to ensure that effective protective action can be taken when this is necessary within a framework of proper safeguards and reasonable opportunities for parents and others connected with the child to challenge such actions before a court. The measures are short-term and time-limited, and may or may not lead to further action under Parts IV or V of the Children Order.

14.2   Trusts are given more positive duties to investigate cases of suspected child abuse and decide what action is appropriate, supported by a new duty on other agencies to give assistance if asked to do so. For emergencies, the place of safety order which could be obtained under section 32 or 99 of the Children and Young Persons Act (Northern Ireland) 1968 is replaced by an emergency protection order with new stricter grounds, clearly defined responsibilities for the person holding the order and shorter time limits.

14.3   An emergency protection order can provide short-term protection where there is a likelihood that a child will suffer significant harm without an order or where access to a child at risk is denied. The order gives the applicant power to remove the child to alternative accommodation or prevent his removal from a safe place, such as a hospital. As its name suggests, the use of the emergency protection order should be confined to situations where there is a real need for urgent action. Nearly every aspect of the new provisions, including the grounds for the order, its effect, opportunities for challenging it and duration, are different.

14.4   The essential features of the new provisions are:

(a)   the court has to be satisfied that the child is likely to suffer significant harm or cannot be seen in circumstances where the child might be suffering significant harm;

(b)   duration is limited to eight days with a possible extension of seven days;

(c) certain persons may apply to discharge the order (to be heard after 72 hours);

(d) the person obtaining the order has limited parental responsibility;

(e) the court may make directions as to contact with the child and/or medical or psychiatric examination or assessment;

(f) in certain circumstances a resident magistrate or a member of the juvenile court panel may make an emergency protection order;

(g) applications may be made in the absence of any other interested parties (ie **ex parte**), and may, with the leave of the clerk of the court, be made orally;

(h) the application must name the child, and where it does not, must describe the child as clearly as possible.

14.5 These key provisions have been limited to what is necessary to protect the child, but it remains an extremely serious step. The grounds for the emergency protection order address more clearly the purpose of having power to remove the child. It must not be regarded - as sometimes was the case with place of safety orders - as a routine response to allegations of child abuse or as a routine first step to initiating care proceedings. The grounds require some evidence that the situation is sufficiently serious to justify such severe powers of intervention being made available. Nevertheless decisive action to protect the child is essential once it appears that the circumstances fall within one of the grounds in Article 63(1). Under Article 66(6) the Trust must apply for an emergency protection order or another of the orders specified if it is refused access to the child or denied information about his whereabouts while carrying out inquiries, unless it is satisfied that the child's welfare can be satisfactorily safeguarded without its taking such action (see paragraph 8.13).

14.6 The duration and effect of the order is limited to what is necessary to protect the child. The parents and certain others will be able to challenge the making of an order if present at the hearing or, if they are not, ask the court to discharge the order after 72 hours.

Removal of the alleged abuser

14.7 Where the need for emergency action centres on alleged abuse of the child the Trust will always want to explore the possibility of providing services to and/or accommodation for the alleged abuser as an alternative to the removal of the child. This could be on a voluntary basis backed up by the provisions of paragraph 6 of Schedule 2 to the Children Order which gives Trusts the discretion to provide assistance with finding alternative housing or cash assistance to the person who leaves the family home. Such practical assistance may be crucial in persuading the alleged abuser to co-operate in this way but should not be viewed as prejudicial to the outcome of inquiries.

14.8 Existing legislation makes no public law provision empowering a court to order an alleged abuser out of the family home. While it is not acceptable for Trusts to avoid their responsibility to apply for an emergency protection order, in certain circumstances private law remedies may be used to achieve the same effect. The Trust should explore these where it is in the child's best interest to do so. The non-abusing parent may agree to apply to the county court for a short-term ouster injunction or to the magistrates' court for an exclusion order under Article 18 of the Domestic Proceedings (Northern Ireland) Order 1980, forcing the alleged abuser out of the home. This may be particularly appropriate in sexual abuse cases where the non-abusing parent has no wish to protect or shield the alleged abuser and where immediate removal of the child is not always in the child's best interests. While keeping the paramount interests of the child uppermost, there needs to be caution with regard to the effect on other relationships in the household.

Who can apply?

14.9 Any person can apply to the court for an emergency protection order. In practice most applications are likely to be made by Trusts or authorised persons although it may sometimes be necessary in dire circumstances for a concerned relative or neighbour, say, to be able to act independently of the statutory authorities in order to protect a child at risk. Court rules require the applicant to notify the Trust, amongst others, of the application, whereupon the Trust's investigation duty under Article 66 comes into play.

CHILDREN ORDER

Emergency Protection Order (Transfer of Responsibilities) Regulations

14.10   The Trust within whose area the child ordinarily resides may take over an emergency protection order obtained by another Trust, individual or organisation if this would be in the child's best interests. The regulations made under Article 71(3) of the Children Order - the Emergency Protection Order (Transfer of Responsibilities) Regulations (see Annex D) - allow the Trust to take over the order, and therefore the powers and responsibility for the child that go with it. In forming its opinion regulation 3 of these regulations requires the Trust to consult with the applicant of the emergency protection order and to consider the following factors:

(a)   the ascertainable wishes and feelings of the child having regard to his age and understanding;

(b)   the child's physical, emotional and educational needs for the duration of the emergency protection order;

(c)   the likely effect on the child of any change in his circumstances which may be caused by a transfer of responsibilities under the order;

(d)   the child's age, sex and family background;

(e)   the circumstances which gave rise to the application for the emergency protection order;

(f)   any directions of the court and other orders made in respect of the child;

(g)   the relationship (if any) of the applicant for the emergency protection order to the child; and

(h)   any plans which the applicant may have in respect of the child.

The intention behind these regulations is to ensure that in an emergency any individual can seek immediate and protective intervention and is not deterred or prevented from doing so by his inability to comply with any or all directions that the court

may make. Applications by an authorised person (ie the NSPCC) are not exempt from these regulations. It is however anticipated that the process of local dialogue and consultation between the NSPCC and the Trust will mean that the transfer powers are rarely exercised without the latter's consent. The regulations will not apply where the child who is subject to an emergency protection order is in a refuge in respect of which there is a certificate issued by the Department of Health and Social Services under Article 70 of the Children Order.

Grounds for application

14.11 The court may only make an emergency protection order if it is satisfied that one of the grounds at Article 63(1)(a), (b) or (c) of the Children Order is satisfied. As with the child assessment order, this condition is emphasised by the words "but only if" in the preamble to paragraph (1). The applicant should not under-estimate this point. In addition to finding the relevant ground in Article 63(1) satisfied, the court must have regard to the fundamental principles in Article 3(1) and (5) of the Order. The welfare of the child must be the paramount consideration and the court must not make an order unless satisfied that this would be better for the child than no order at all. The court is not required to have regard to the checklist in Article 3(3) as the emergency nature of the application and its limited duration make this impracticable.

14.12 The three different grounds at Article 63(1)(a), (b) and (c) deal with different situations. It is easiest to consider the grounds at Article 63(1)(b) and (c) first. These are discussed below. The grounds at Article 63(1)(a) are discussed at paragraph 14.19.

14.13 Article 63(1)(b) provides for an application by a Trust in particular circumstances - where, because it has reasonable cause to suspect that a child in its area is suffering, or is likely to suffer, significant harm, the Trust is carrying out inquiries under Article 66(1)(b) and those inquiries are being frustrated by access to the child being unreasonably refused, and it has reasonable cause to believe that access to the child is required as a matter of urgency. Although this ground applies only to a Trust, persons from other voluntary or statutory agencies may be acting on the Trust's behalf to undertake the inquiries.

14.14 The grounds at Article 63(1)(c) provide for an application in the same circumstances by an authorised person (as defined by Article 49(2)) who has been making inquiries except that he must also satisfy the court as to his reasonable cause for suspicion.

14.15 The circumstances in which these 'frustrated access' grounds are to be used must be distinguished from the child assessment order. They are for use in an emergency (where access is required as a matter of urgency) where enquiries cannot be completed because the child cannot be seen but there is enough cause to suspect the child is suffering or likely to suffer significant harm. The child assessment order applies where there is a need for further investigation of the child's health and development but he is not thought to be in immediate danger.

14.16 The hypothesis of the grounds at Article 63(1)(b) and (c) is that this combination of factors is evidence of an emergency or the likelihood of an emergency. The court will have to decide whether the refusal of access to the child was unreasonable in the circumstances. It might consider a refusal unreasonable if the person refusing had explained to him the reason for the enquiries and the request for access, the request itself was reasonable, and he had failed to respond positively in some other suitable way - by arranging for the child to be seen immediately by his GP, for example. Refusal of a request to see a sleeping child in the middle of the night may not be unreasonable, but refusal to allow access at a reasonable time without good reason could well be. The parent who refuses immediate access but offers to take the child to a local clinic the following morning may not be making a reasonable refusal where the risk to the child is believed to be imminent or where previous voluntary arrangements have broken down.

14.17 A person authorised to seek access is defined in Article 63(2)(b). In the case of a Trust a person authorised to seek access means an officer of the Trust or a person authorised to make enquiries on the Trust's behalf. In the case of the NSPCC it means an officer of that organisation. A person seeking access must produce evidence of his authority if asked to do so (Article 63(3)) and failure to comply may well make a refusal to allow access reasonable. As a matter of good practice any professional practitioner seeking access to a child should show evidence of his authority whether asked to do so or not.

14.18   The Trust is required by Article 66(6) to respond positively to a refusal of access or a denial of information about the child's whereabouts when it is conducting inquiries: it must apply for an emergency protection order or take other specified action unless satisfied that such action is unnecessary. These conditions for an emergency protection order reflect the importance of seeing the child when there are concerns about his welfare. The potential significance of unreasonable refusal of access for the child's welfare in suspicious circumstances is fully recognised in the grounds at Article 63(1)(b) and (c), and there is now no justification for failing to act because of lack of information occasioned by inability to see the child. If the court makes an emergency protection order under condition (b) or (c), and it considers that adequate information as to the child's whereabouts is not available to the applicant but is available to someone else, such as the person who was last known to be looking after the child, it can require that person in the order to disclose information about the child's whereabouts (Article 67(1)). It can also authorise entry to premises to search for the child (Article 67(3)) or other children (Article 67(4)) (see paragraphs 14.31-14.36).

14.19   The other condition under which an emergency protection order may be made, at Article 63(1)(a), is more of a general purpose provision for emergencies. For the criteria to be met the court must be satisfied that there is reasonable cause to believe that the child is likely to suffer significant harm:

(a)   if he is not removed to accommodation provided by or on behalf of the applicant; or

(b)   if the child does not remain in the place in which he is being accommodated.

There is a clear distinction to be made in relation to the significant harm test in Article 63(1)(a) as against sub-paragraphs (b) and (c) discussed above. In the former it is the **court** that must have reasonable cause to believe; in the latter it is the **applicant** who must have reasonable cause to suspect. The term "significant harm" in this context has the same meaning as it does in relation to care proceedings (see paragraphs 9.17-9.27).

14.20   The condition at Article 63(1)(a) is for cases where the child has been seen, or seeing him may not be relevant, for example where a baby has just been born into a family with a long history of violent behaviour to young children. The Trust may be carrying out inquiries under Article 66 or in response to a direction under Article 56, for example, and may have been refused access to the child. The test in relation to significant harm looks to the future. In other words, it may be necessary to remove the child or keep the child where he is, in order to protect him from the likelihood of suffering significant harm. For the grounds under this sub-paragraph to be satisfied significant harm must be likely. Evidence of harm which was occurring at the time of the application or has occurred in the past is not sufficient unless it indicates that harm is likely to occur in the near future. Unlike the requirement of previous legislation, there does not have to have been previous harm for the order to be made.

14.21   There are a number of additional points to be emphasised:

(a)   in deciding whether to grant an emergency protection order on this ground the court will wish to know what it is that necessitates urgent action, whether, if removal of the child is necessary, it can be achieved with the co-operation of the parents and the provision of accommodation and whether a decision can wait until the parents have had an opportunity to properly prepare their case at an interim hearing. The applicant will be expected to give as much of this information as possible either orally or in the application form for the order. One of the reasons that this approach is necessary is because of the no order principle in Article 3(5) of the Children Order;

(b)   the court may take account of any statement contained in any report made to the court in the course of, or in connection with, the hearing or any evidence given during the hearing which the court believes to be relevant to the application. This enables the court to give such weight as it thinks appropriate to health visiting or social work records, medical reports, opinions and any relevant hearsay (Article 64(6)).

CHILDREN ORDER

14.22 As with all orders under the Children Order, even where the above conditions apply, the court will not automatically make an emergency protection order. It must still consider the welfare principle and the presumption of no order. In most cases it is unlikely that the parents will be present at the hearing. With only one side of the case before it the court will want to examine very carefully the information it is given, especially where the basis of the application is likelihood of future harm or inability to see the child. It may be that the initial order will be made for a very short time such as the next available hearing date so that an extension to the order will be on notice to parents and others.

Application procedure

14.23 Anyone can apply for an emergency protection order on the first ground (Article 63(1)(a)) which concerns the likelihood of significant harm, including a Trust or an authorised person. Only a Trust or an authorised person can apply for an order on the remaining grounds (Article 63(1)(b) or (c)) which concern the denial of access to the child. "Anyone" could include a concerned relative, a neighbour or a teacher.

14.24 The Children (Allocation of Proceedings) Order (Northern Ireland) 1996 provides that an application for an emergency protection order is to be made to a family proceedings court and it is one of the few proceedings which cannot be transferred to a higher court. The Magistrates' Courts (Children (Northern Ireland) Order 1995) Rules (Northern Ireland) 1996 will govern applications under the Children Order in magistrates' courts (including family proceedings courts). They provide that an application for an emergency protection order may be made **ex parte** - that is, without other persons having to be given notice of the hearing and allowed to attend and make representations. Those rules also provide that an **ex parte** application for an emergency protection order may be made to a resident magistrate or a member of the lay panel sitting alone. This is only intended for urgent applications which arise outside normal court hours.

14.25 The rules of court provide for applications to be heard **inter partes** (at a full hearing with others who wish to attend if able to

do so) but the very fact that the situation is considered to be an emergency requiring immediate action will make this inappropriate or impracticable in most cases. However, if a court is available the application, including **ex parte** applications, should be made to a court. It should be borne in mind that in certain instances to put the parents on notice of the application might place the child in greater danger. Early morning removal of children should only take place where there are clear grounds for believing significant harm would otherwise be caused to the child or vital evidence is only obtainable by such means.

14.26 Because of the emergency nature of the application and because most applications will be heard **ex parte**, rules of court require the applicant, rather than the court, to serve a copy of the application and the order within 48 hours on the parties to the proceedings, any person who is not a party but has actual care of the child and the Trust in whose area the child is normally resident if that Trust is not the applicant. Notice of the application must also be given to a parent. The need to inform parents of their rights and responsibilities under the new order is seen as crucial. Explanatory notes will be served with a copy of the order informing parents in easily understood language of what will happen to their child and what they can do next. These notes are printed on the back of the emergency protection order.

Effects of an emergency protection order

14.27 While an emergency protection order is in force there are three effects. It operates as a direction to any person who is in a position to do so to comply with any request to produce the child to the applicant; authorises removal to, or prevention of, removal from accommodation provided by or on behalf of the applicant and it gives parental responsibility to the applicant (Article 63(4)). However, the applicant's parental responsibility is restricted to taking whatever action is reasonably required to safeguard and promote the child's welfare in the short term (Article 63(5) and paragraph 14.37).

Directions as to disclosure of a child's whereabouts

14.28 In situations where persons looking after the child do not readily

agree to hand the child over, the emergency protection order provides a formal direction to any person who is in a position to do so to comply with any request to produce the child to the applicant (Article 63(4)(a)).

14.29 If the applicant for an emergency protection order does not know the whereabouts of a child, but that information seems to be available to another person, the court may require that person to disclose the information when requested to do so by the applicant (Article 67(1)). Disclosure must be made to the applicant on request rather than the court. This provision is intended to ensure that access to the child is not frustrated because information is being withheld from the applicant. The named person (or persons - the order may cite more than one person) will normally be the person who has previously refused to disclose the information to the applicant and appears to the court to be in possession of the information, although the court may in theory name anyone. It would be advisable to ask courts as a matter of routine to attach this direction to an emergency protection order to avoid unnecessary returns to court in those cases where it is not known for sure that the child is at particular premises.

14.30 No one shall be excused from complying with a direction for disclosure made under Article 67(1) on the grounds that it may incriminate himself or his spouse, and "a statement or admission made in complying shall not be admissible in evidence against either of them in any proceedings for any offence other than perjury" (Article 67(2)). This is intended to encourage witnesses to give evidence and provide vital information, and to avoid delay in children's cases. Failure to comply with the direction would be contempt of court.

Powers of entry

14.31 The Children Order gives the courts powers to authorise an applicant such as a social worker to enter and search premises for a child who is the subject of an emergency protection order (Article 67(3)). Applicants may ask for this authority in cases where difficulties are anticipated. This authorisation may be given when the court makes the order, and will specify which premises may be entered and searched, and by whom. The

child will be the child named or described in the order (see paragraphs 14.35 and 14.36 on supporting warrants).

14.32 If the applicant believes there may be another child at risk in the premises to be searched, he may ask the court for authority to search for that child also (Article 67(4)). Where the applicant cannot name the child, the child should be described as clearly as possible in the order.

14.33 If on searching the premises the second child is found and the applicant believes that there are sufficient grounds for making an emergency protection order, the order authorising the search for the second child may be treated as an emergency protection order (Article 67(5)). The authorised person must notify the court of the result of the search; ie whether the child was found and if so, what action was taken or is planned. The court should be told whether the authority to search for the child is now being treated as an emergency protection order. If so, and if the applicant for the order is not the Trust, the applicant will need to inform the Trust accordingly so that it can fulfil its duty to investigate the child's circumstances under Article 66. If the child is not found then the provisions of Articles 68 and 69 apply, dealing with the abduction and recovery of children.

14.34 This provision is intended to cover the situation where the applicant believes there may be more than one child in the family or on the premises who is likely to suffer significant harm. In most cases the applicant will know if there are other children and should, if there are grounds, apply for an emergency protection order for each child. There may be occasions, however, when the applicant cannot identify the specific child but wants to check on the child or children in the same circumstances as the child for whom the emergency protection order is sought. Although an order under Article 67(4) is quite distinct from an emergency protection order, the need for it arises out of the same circumstances. It is for this reason and to avoid any unnecessary delay that an application for an order under Article 67(4) has been incorporated in the application form for an emergency protection order so that, where appropriate, the two orders can be applied for and made simultaneously.

14.35 It is a criminal offence to intentionally obstruct an authorised

person exercising his powers of entry and search under Article 67(3) and (4). If this does occur, or is anticipated, the court can issue a warrant authorising any constable to assist the authorised person in entering and searching the named premises (Article 67(9)). The authorised person may accompany the constable if he wishes, although the court may direct otherwise (Article 67(10)(b)). In practice where it is the Trust or NSPCC who is the applicant the social worker would normally accompany the constable, as he will be responsible for the child when the child has been removed from the premises, and it is desirable to reduce the number of officials whom the child encounters in what will certainly be a very traumatic and difficult time. Any warrant which the court issues to the constable may direct that, if he chooses, the constable may be accompanied by a medical practitioner, registered nurse or registered health visitor (Article 67(11)). It would be good practice always to request such a direction. The authorised person, if qualified to do so by virtue of his knowledge of the child, the family and the circumstances leading up to the application for the order, should advise the constable whether such a person is available if needed. The warrant will authorise the constable to use reasonable force if necessary in order to assist the applicant in the exercise of his powers to enter and search the premises for the child (Article 67(9)).

14.36 When making an application for an emergency protection order, the applicant should consider whether at the same time he needs to apply for a warrant for a constable to be brought in to assist in the exercise of emergency protection orders powers. This will of course depend upon the circumstances of the case, and the applicant's knowledge and previous experience of the people with whom he will be dealing. However, the emergency nature of the case should always be borne in mind; if any difficulties in gaining entry are foreseen, or if the applicant believes that he is likely to be threatened, intimidated or physically prevented from carrying out this part of the order, the possibility of simultaneously obtaining a warrant should always be considered. If necessary the advice of the police should be sought when considering such an application. In dire emergencies the police can exercise their powers under Article 19(1)(e) of the Police and Criminal Evidence (Northern Ireland) Order 1989 to enter and search premises without a warrant for the purpose of saving life and limb. Similarly under Article

27(3)(e) of the Police and Criminal Evidence (Northern Ireland) Order 1989 the police may arrest without a warrant any person who has committed any offence where the arrest is necessary to protect the child from that person.

Removal of the child

14.37 The emergency protection order gives the applicant parental responsibility for the child but this is limited insofar as the applicant is authorised to exercise his powers to remove or prevent removal (from a safe place) only in order to safeguard and promote the welfare of the child. If an applicant gains access and finds the child is not harmed and is not likely to suffer significant harm he may not remove the child (Article 63(5)). If removal is necessary, the child is entitled to an explanation appropriate to his age and understanding of why he is being taken away from home and what will happen to him, even though as a party the older child or his solicitor or guardian *ad litem* will receive a copy of the application and order. A duty to explain to the child is laid on the designated police officer when taking a child into police protection (see paragraph 16.4).

Return of the child

14.38 When an emergency protection order is in force and the applicant has already removed the child, or prevented the child's removal from accommodation, the applicant is under a duty to return the child or, as the case may be, allow the child to be removed if it appears to him that it is safe for the child to be returned or removed (Article 63(10)). Where the applicant is satisfied that it is safe for the child to be returned, the applicant is under a duty to return the child to the care of the person from whose care he was removed (Article 63(11)(a)). If that is not reasonably practicable the applicant must instead return the child to the care of a parent, any person who is not a parent of the child but has parental responsibility for him, or such person as the applicant considers appropriate. However, in this latter situation the agreement of the court must be sought (Article 63(11)(b)).

CHILDREN ORDER

14.39 If, after the child has been returned, there is again cause for concern, the applicant may exercise his powers under the emergency protection order and remove the child once more, if it appears to the applicant that a change in the child's circumstances makes it necessary to do so. This possibility should always be made clear to the parents where a child has been returned and the emergency protection order has not yet expired. In this situation the original duration of the emergency protection order is not extended and therefore the order would expire at the due date (Article 63(12)). It is an offence to intentionally obstruct any person exercising his power (under Article 63(4)(b)) to remove, or prevent the removal of, a child.

Additional directions

14.40 Where the court makes an emergency protection order it has the discretion to give additional directions as to the contact the child must be allowed to have with certain persons and may be allowed to have with any other named person (Article 63(6)(a)). The court direction may impose conditions (Article 63(8)). However, subject to these, there is a general duty on the applicant under Article 63(13) to allow the child reasonable contact with his parents, any person who is not a parent but has parental responsibility, any person with whom he was living before the order was made, any person in whose favour a contact order is in force with respect to the child (under Article 8), any person who is allowed contact by virtue of an order under Article 53 or anyone acting on behalf of any of these persons. The court may give directions regarding contact not only when the emergency protection order is made, but also at any time while it is in force and the court may also vary the directions at any time (Article 63(9)). The persons who are able to apply for a variation are prescribed by the rules of court.

14.41 It is anticipated that where the applicant is a Trust the court will leave contact to the discretion of the Trust or order that reasonable contact be negotiated between the parties unless the issue is disputed, in which case specific directions can be sought at a hearing. In considering what is reasonable contact the Trust will need to explore fully the wishes and feelings of the child. The Trust may wish to limit contact or seek directions to control

contact with families it believes to be troublesome and who are likely to upset the child or where there are allegations of sexual abuse and the contact needs to be supervised. In these circumstances, the Trust should seek a direction defining contact. Where a direction has been made to define contact the Trust will need to inform other agencies who may have regular dealings with the child, for example, the school the child attends.

14.42 The court may also give directions about any medical or psychiatric examination or other assessment of the child (Article 63(6)(b)), and may specify which types of examination or assessment should not be made unless the court directs otherwise (Article 63(8)). In promoting the welfare of the child the court can therefore ensure that he is not subjected to unnecessary assessments. As a matter of good practice a Trust should always seek directions on assessment or examination of the child where this is likely to be an issue. Where possible it is anticipated that assessments will be undertaken by professionals agreed between the parties or arranged by the guardian *ad litem*. The court may direct, and the parents, if present, may request that the child's GP observe or participate in the assessment. Whether or not parents had an opportunity to challenge the making of a direction for a medical assessment they may wish to apply for it to be varied.

14.43 The court may give directions regarding medical or psychiatric examination or other assessment of the child not only when the emergency protection order is made, but also at any time while it is in force and the court may also vary the directions at any time. Where such directions are given, the child may, if he is of sufficient understanding to make an informed decision, refuse to submit to the examination or other assessment (Article 63(7)). The consequences of such a refusal are discussed in paragraphs 10.17 and 10.18.

Duration

14.44 In the first instance an emergency protection order may be granted for up to eight days beginning with the day on which it is made (Article 64(1)). However, by virtue of section 39(4) of the Interpretation Act (Northern Ireland) 1954, when the time

limit for doing an act expires on a Sunday or a public holiday, the act may be done on the next following day that is not a Sunday or public holiday. This will exclude a Sunday or public holiday from the calculation of the eight-day period when such days fall on the eighth day. Where the child is in police protection and a Trust applies for an emergency protection order the period of eight days of any emergency protection order granted starts from the date that the child was taken into police protection and not from the date of the emergency protection order application (Article 64(2)).

Extensions

14.45 The court may extend the period of the emergency protection order once only (Article 64(5)) and for a period of up to seven days (including public holidays and Sundays). Court rules require an application for an extension to be made on notice in a full **inter partes** hearing by any person who has parental responsibility for the child as a result of an emergency protection order (ie only a Trust or authorised person), and is entitled to apply for a care order with respect to the child (Article 64(3)). However, the court may only extend the period of the order if it has reasonable cause to believe that the child concerned is likely to suffer significant harm if the order is not extended (Article 64(4)). If there has been a genuine emergency and the Trust believes care proceedings should follow it should normally be possible to proceed to satisfy the court as to the grounds for an interim order within the first period. If an extension is sought the court will want to be satisfied as to the reasons for the delay.

Appeals

14.46 There is no right of appeal against the making or refusal to make an emergency protection order, the extension of, or refusal to extend, an emergency protection order, the discharge of, or refusal to discharge, an emergency protection order or the giving of, or refusal to give, directions in connection with an emergency protection order. However, despite the short duration of the order, there are opportunities available to challenge the making of an order and directions may be varied on application.

Discharges

14.47   No application for the discharge of an emergency protection order shall be heard by the court before the expiry of the period of 72 hours beginning with the making of the order. This will not prevent applications for discharge being made before 72 hours are up. A range of persons may apply to the court for an emergency protection order to be discharged. These are; the child, a parent of the child, any person who is not a parent but who has parental responsibility and any person with whom the child was living before the making of the order. However, an application to discharge an emergency protection order will not be allowed:

(a)   where a person who would otherwise be entitled to apply for the emergency protection order to be discharged was given notice in accordance with rules of court of the hearing at which the order was made and was present at the hearing;

(b)   where an emergency protection order has been extended in duration for a period not exceeding seven days (Article 64(10)). However, in this latter case, the decision to extend the duration of the order can only be made at an **inter partes** hearing so there would be an opportunity for representations to be made that there should be no extension.

14.48   The 72-hour provision will give parents and those listed in paragraph 14.47 an opportunity to clarify any confusion that may have arisen from the making of the order or any directions in their absence. It will also give them time to prepare their case should they wish to challenge the making of the order. It is not intended that 72 hours will become the effective time limit by which the Trust must complete its assessment if it is to contest an application to discharge the order. The Trust will be expected to go as far and as fast as is reasonably practicable in undertaking the assessment. If an application comes to court for the discharge of an order after 72 hours and the assessment has not been completed, the Trust will advise the court accordingly and unless circumstances have so changed as to allay any concerns the Trust may have had for the safety of the child, it is unlikely that the court will agree to discharge the emergency protection order.

CHILDREN ORDER

Child in refuge

14.49   Whilst a child is at a refuge, within the meaning of Article 70 of the Children Order, the organisation may apply for an emergency protection order under Article 63(1) or ask the police to take the child into police protection under Article 65. The grounds to be satisfied are that the organisation believes that the child is likely to suffer significant harm if the child does not remain where he is.

CHILDREN ORDER

CHAPTER 15: CHILD ASSESSMENT ORDERS

15.1   The child assessment order, established by Article 62, deals with the single issue of enabling an assessment of the child to be made where significant harm is suspected but the child is not thought to be at immediate risk, the applicant considers that an assessment is required and the parents or other persons responsible for the child have refused to co-operate.

15.2   Its purpose is to allow a Trust or authorised person to ascertain enough about the state of the child's health or development or the way in which the child has been treated to decide what further action, if any, is required. It is less interventionist than the emergency protection order, interim care order and interim supervision order and should not be used where the circumstances of the case suggest that one of these orders would be more appropriate. The court has power to make an emergency protection order instead of the child assessment order if, after hearing the evidence, it considers that the circumstances warrant this (Article 62(4)). Parents and children should be made aware that an application for a child assessment order may result in the court making an emergency protection order.

15.3   The child assessment order is emphatically not for emergencies. It is a lesser, heavily court-controlled order dealing with the narrow issue of examination or assessment of the child in specific circumstances of non co-operation by the parents and lack of evidence of the need for a different type of order or other action.

15.4   Proceedings under Part VI are not classified as family proceedings for the purpose of the Children Order. This means that in these proceedings the court must either make, or refuse to make, the order applied for and cannot make any other kind of order. The only exception is the court's specific authority to make an emergency protection order instead of a child assessment order.

15.5   The chapter uses references to 'parents' in relation to the carers of children in respect of whom orders under Part VI may be sought, but it applies equally to carers even though such persons will often not have parental responsibility.

CHILDREN ORDER

Who may apply?

15.6   Only a Trust or authorised person may apply for a child
        assessment order; in this limitation it is similar to care and
        supervision orders but not emergency protection orders, for
        which anyone may apply to the court (see paragraph 14.23).
        The court has to be satisfied on each of the following three
        conditions:

   (a)   that the applicant has reasonable cause to suspect that
          the child is suffering, or is likely to suffer, significant harm;

   (b)   that an assessment of the state of the child's health or
          development, or of the way he has been treated, is
          required to enable the applicant to determine whether or
          not the child is suffering, or is likely to suffer, significant
          harm; and

   (c)   that it is unlikely that such an assessment will be made, or
          be satisfactory, in the absence of a child assessment
          order.

        In addition to the conditions laid down for the making of a child
        assessment order, the court must have regard to the
        paramountcy of the child's welfare (Article 3(1)) and the no
        order principle (Article 3(5)). The court is not required to
        consider the welfare check-list (Article 3(3)), although it is
        expected to consider factors from the check-list where
        appropriate.

Conditions to be satisfied

15.7   The principal conditions are very specific. The order is for cases
        where there are suspicions, but no firm evidence, of actual or
        likely significant harm in circumstances which do not constitute
        an emergency; the applicant considers that a decisive step to
        obtain an assessment is needed to show whether the concern is
        well-founded or further action is not required, and that informal
        arrangements to have such an assessment carried out have
        failed. For example, the parents or other persons looking after
        the child have resisted attempts to arrange an examination or
        assessment by agreement or failed to bring the child to see a

doctor when arrangements have been made, and have not made suitable alternative arrangements. The problem may have come to light from contact with the family or child by a health visitor, social worker, doctor, teacher or other professional, or from a concerned relative or neighbour.

15.8 A child assessment order will usually be most appropriate where the harm to the child is long-term and cumulative rather than sudden and severe. The circumstances may be nagging concern about a child who appears to be failing to thrive; or the parents are ignorant of, or unwilling to face up to, possible harm to their child because of the state of his health or development; or it appears that the child may be subject to wilful neglect or abuse but not to such an extent as to place him at serious immediate risk. Sexual abuse, which covers a wide range of behaviour, can fall into this category. The harm to the child can be long-term rather than immediate and it does not necessarily require emergency action. However, emergency action should not be avoided where disclosure of the abuse is itself likely to put the child at immediate risk of significant harm and/or where there is an urgent need to gather particular forensic evidence which would not otherwise be forthcoming in relation to the likelihood of significant harm.

15.9 One of the essential ingredients for a child assessment order is that an assessment is needed to help establish basic facts about the child's condition. Because information is lacking it is unlikely that an interim care or supervision order could be obtained and an examination or assessment arranged under those provisions: the condition for an interim order - "reasonable grounds for believing that the circumstances are as mentioned in Article 50(2)" - Article 57(2) (see paragraphs 10.1 and 10.2) is more demanding and would be difficult to satisfy. However, the applicant should know enough of the circumstances to satisfy himself that the child is not in immediate danger; if possible the child should have been seen recently by someone competent to judge this. A skilled social work practitioner would be in a position to make a judgement as to the child's emotional state and to obvious changes in the child's physical well-being. Finer judgements, particularly in relation to very young children, may require input from the child's health visitor, GP or other health professional. Refusal to allow a child about whom there is serious concern to be seen

(as opposed to being examined or assessed) can be a classic sign of a potential emergency, and will require the response of an application for an emergency protection order under the 'frustrated access' condition (see paragraphs 14.13-14.18 on Article 63(1)(b) and (c)).

Prior investigations

15.10 An application by a Trust should always be preceded by an investigation under Article 66 (see Chapter 8). Since the order is for non-emergencies, there will be no justification for the investigation to be merely superficial. The court considering an application for a child assessment order will expect to be given details of the investigation and how it arose, including, in particular, details of the applicant's attempts to satisfy himself as to the welfare of the child by arrangement with the persons caring for him (see paragraph 15.25). If the court is not satisfied that all reasonable efforts were made to persuade them to co-operate and that these were resisted, the application is likely to founder on the third condition of Article 62(1).

Commencement and duration

15.11 The assessment must be completed within seven days unless the court specifies a shorter period (Article 62(5)). The order must specify the date by which the assessment is to begin. There is no right to apply for an extension if it is not completed within this period and it is not possible to apply for a second order within six months without the leave of the court (Article 179(15)).

15.12 The applicant should make the necessary arrangements in advance of the application, so that it would usually be possible to complete within such a period an initial multi-disciplinary assessment of the child's medical, intellectual, emotional, social and behavioural needs. This should be sufficient to establish whether the child is suffering, or likely to suffer, significant harm and, if so, what further action is required. Trusts will need to review with the appropriate agencies in their area, the necessary procedures to be complied with to ensure that an assessment can be undertaken satisfactorily within the intentions and time

limit of this part of the legislation. The applicant should be able to give details of the proposed arrangements to the court so that it may consider these when giving directions.

Effect of order

15.13   The child assessment order has two main effects. Firstly, it imposes a duty on any person who is in a position to produce the child - usually a person having parental responsibility for the child or the person having care of the child at the time the order is made - to produce him to the person named in the order so that the assessment may take place, and to comply with any directions or other requirements included in the order (Article 62(6)). Secondly, it authorises any person carrying out the assessment, or part of it, to do so in accordance with the terms of the order (Article 62(7)). Unlike the emergency protection order or interim or full care order, the holder of the order does not acquire parental responsibility for the child. A child of sufficient understanding to make an informed decision may refuse to consent to the assessment. The guardian *ad litem* may well be able to advise the court as to whether the child is of sufficient understanding to make such a decision. In performing this duty the guardian *ad litem* may need to seek the assistance of professionals in other disciplines, and particularly where a child suffers from a handicap which impairs his ability to communicate. The guardian *ad litem* will wish to explore with the child his reluctance to undertake an assessment, and advise the court accordingly. Providing the child with further advice may result in the child withdrawing his opposition, but all professionals should take particular care to avoid coercing the child into agreement even where there is a belief that the refusal to comply is itself the product of coercion by a parent, relative or friend.

Directions

15.14   The court should take advice from those presenting the case, and, if necessary, other professionals involved in the case (including the guardian *ad litem*) about what the assessment should cover, and may make directions accordingly (this may be based on information from any prior investigation under Article

66). This may include, for example, whether it should be limited to a medical examination or cover other aspects of the child's health and development, and by whom and where it should be conducted. It may require that the child's usual doctor or another medical professional may participate and, for example, for the child's parents' medical representative to be present. The court may also make directions relating to the assessment of the child as seems appropriate and in the child's interest (Article 62(6)(b)). The court should be asked to include in the order details of those to whom results of the assessment should be given.

Child away from home

15.15 Article 62(9) provides for keeping the child away from home for the purposes of the assessment. This is intended to be a reserve provision, and, if used, the number of overnight stays should be kept as low as possible. The assessment should be conducted with as little trauma for the child and parents as possible. It is important that the child assessment order is not regarded as a variant of the emergency protection order with its removal power. The purposes of the two orders are quite different. The child may only be kept away from home in the circumstances specified, namely:

(a)   the court is satisfied that it is necessary for the purposes of the assessment; and

(b)   it is done in accordance with directions specified in the order; and it is limited to such period or periods (which need not be the full period of the order) specified in the order.

The need for an overnight stay might arise if the child were thought to have special needs or characteristics which necessitated overnight observation. It might be difficult to argue that an overnight stay "is necessary for the purposes of the assessment" simply because the arrangements made for the assessment would require the child to travel very early or very late; the arrangements made by the applicant should aim to avoid difficulties of this kind. However, in exceptional circumstances, either for medical or social work reasons, an

overnight stay might facilitate the completion of the assessment. Examples might include where the child has eating difficulties, seriously disturbed sleep patterns or other symptoms that would require 24-hour continuous observation and monitoring.

15.16 If the court directs that the child may be kept away from home, it must also give directions as it thinks fit about the contact the child must have with other persons during this period. A temporary overnight stay cannot be equated with being placed in care, but the court may well be guided on contact by the presumption of reasonable contact between a child in care and his parents, guardian and certain other persons established by Article 53 (see Chapter 12). It would also want to consider requests to be allowed contact from other persons who have to be notified of the hearing. The court may consider that the parents or other persons closely connected with the child should be allowed to stay with the child overnight, and the applicant for the order should consider offering this facility when asking for a direction that the child be kept away from home. As for all questions affecting the child that arise under the Children Order, the court must give paramount consideration to the child's welfare when considering contact and in doing so will wish to ascertain the views and feelings of the child. The guardian *ad litem* should also be able to assist in this respect.

Grounds for emergency protection order

15.17 The court is specifically required not to make a child assessment order if it is satisfied that there are grounds for making an emergency protection order and that it ought to make such an order instead of a child assessment order (Article 62(4)). In that event, it may treat the application as an application for an emergency protection order and proceed under Articles 63 and 64. The court may decide on hearing the evidence that the child's situation is more serious than the applicant judged, or new information indicating an emergency may emerge from the guardian *ad litem's* inquiries or other evidence. Although the different grounds and effect clearly distinguish the child assessment order for non-emergencies and the emergency protection order for emergencies, this power has been given to the court to guard against expressed fears that some applicants might opt for the less serious order when in reality the full

powers of the emergency protection order are required.

15.18   Parents and children should be made aware that an application for a child assessment order may result in the court making an emergency protection order. Trusts and authorised persons should ensure that all staff concerned with investigations of this kind receive proper training in the correct use of these quite different orders and that applications for all court orders benefit from timely legal advice. The failure to act decisively due to an optimistic view of the impact of the child assessment order powers might in some circumstances have very serious consequences for the child concerned.

Other procedural requirements

15.19   Procedural requirements are outlined in Article 62(11) and (12) and detailed more fully in the rules of court. They reflect the non-emergency nature of the order. The application should always be considered on notice at a full hearing in which the parties are able to participate. Therefore the application may be challenged at that stage. The rules of court provide for the circumstances in which and by whom an application to vary or discharge a child assessment order may be made. Again, unlike the emergency protection order, there is a right of appeal against the making, or the court's refusal to make, a child assessment order. Where an application has been made for a child assessment order, whether successful or otherwise, no further application can be made by particular persons (this includes a Trust) within six months without the leave of the court (Article 179(15)). In addition, when disposing of an application, the court has a general power under Article 179(14) to order that no further application may be made at any time without the leave of the court. This power is designed to curb the activities of the vexatious litigant and is unlikely to be invoked against a Trust properly exercising its duty to protect children.

Failure to produce child

15.20   The applicant should be prepared for the possibility that the persons responsible for the child fail to produce him for the

assessment in accordance with the order. Immediate inquiries should be made to establish whether there is a satisfactory explanation for non-production of the child. For example, the child or the person caring for him may have been taken ill, or the requirements of the order may have been misunderstood. In circumstances like these, the person concerned should if possible be persuaded to comply immediately, otherwise the court should be asked to vary the terms of the order. Deliberate refusal to comply must add to concern for the child's welfare and would probably be sufficient to satisfy the significant harm or frustrated access conditions for an emergency protection order (see paragraphs 14.13-14.18 on Article 63(1)(b) and (c). If the developing circumstances make the case so urgent that there is not time to apply for an emergency protection order, the police should be asked to use their powers under Article 65 of the Children Order to take the child into police protection. These can only be exercised, however, where access is not an obstacle and the police can in effect "find" the child since there are no powers of search attached to Article 65. In dire emergencies and for the purpose of saving life or limb, the police have reserve powers under Article 19(1)(e) of the Police and Criminal Evidence (Northern Ireland) Order 1989 to enter and search premises without a warrant.

15.21 The potential significance of non-production for the child's welfare should not be underestimated; a person who had been abusing the child may be prepared to go to extreme lengths to prevent the child being seen or assessed. If the court considers when hearing the application for the child assessment order that there is a real danger that the order will not be complied with, it may, if the grounds for the greater order are satisfied, feel able to exercise its power to make an emergency protection order instead. Where there was insufficient information at an earlier stage to justify an application for an interim care or supervision order, non-production of the child for assessment would not be likely to add sufficiently to the evidence to make an application for either of those orders successful.

Child assessment orders and family proceedings

15.22 A child assessment order can subsist alongside an Article 8 order or an education supervision order, but would not be

required where a care order, emergency protection order or supervision order was in force. Under a care order, the Trust would be able to arrange an assessment without specific court authority. If parents object, the Trust would have to use its powers under Article 52(3)(b) to restrict the parents' exercise of their parental responsibility. Under a supervision order, the court could be asked to provide for an assessment in the order or give directions on the subject. Under an emergency protection order the court has specific direction powers concerning examination and assessment. Although the holder of an emergency protection order has power to arrange for an examination, to avoid disputes, in view of the short period during which the order has effect, the court should be asked to use its direction powers. In all these circumstances the child of sufficient understanding may refuse to submit to an examination or assessment.

Result of the assessment

15.23   Once the assessment is complete it is for the applicant to decide what action, if any, to take next. The applicant is not obliged to report back to the court but may be required to provide others with results of the assessment. Should information of a criminal nature come to light during the assessment, the police will need to be involved and decisions made about when and with whom the results of the assessment are shared. If the child is kept away from home for the purposes of the assessment and so serious a situation is revealed by the assessment that the child cannot be allowed to return home, an emergency protection order should be sought. Given the purpose of the child assessment order, it is anticipated that any follow-up will usually be through the provision of services for the child and the family. The Trust or authorised person will need to consider what action to take in the light of the results of the assessment. Since it may not have been possible to conduct a comprehensive assessment within the period of the order, the findings may show that the child's health and development is being impaired but not identify the problem in full or be conclusive as to treatment.

15.24   The Trust should consider whether further assessment is required and, if so, explore whether this can be arranged on a voluntary basis with the parents - who may have been persuaded by the

child assessment order to be more positive - or should be persuaded by way of an application for an interim care order or interim supervision order. The Trust will have to consider whether the grounds for such an order would be satisfied. Where the initial assessment reveals a clear picture of the child's health and development and shows impairment which should not be ignored, the issue will be whether the child's welfare can be safeguarded and promoted by the provision of services under Part IV of the Children Order. Parents who are willing, but may not be coping adequately, may be helped by services of the kind to be provided under paragraphs 5, 9 and 10 of Schedule 2 to the Children Order. Alternatively, it might be best for the child to be provided with accommodation away from home for a period under Article 21 while the parents are assisted.

Practice issues

15.25 A number of important practice issues arise. One is that as far as possible the child assessment order should be used sparingly. Although a lesser order than others in Parts V and VI of the Children Order, it still represents substantial intervention in the upbringing of the child and could lead to yet further intervention. It should be contemplated only where there is reason for serious concern for the child. It should not be used for a child whose parents are reluctant to use the normal child health services. There should have been a substantial effort to persuade those caring for the child of the need for an assessment and to persuade them to agree to suitable arrangements voluntarily. When an assessment order is obtained it will be necessary for the parents to work with professional practitioners, and their co-operation during the process is essential if there is to be a useful assessment on which to base future action. A Trust will need to be sensitive to issues of gender, race and culture when formulating arrangements for an assessment. The parents may resist making the child available to Trust appointed professionals but may be amenable to either the family doctor or an independent professional examining, or participating in the examination of the child. Arrangements of this kind may well provide sufficient information about the child's welfare and therefore should not be rejected by a Trust out of hand. **If such arrangements were considered as satisfactory by the court hearing an**

application for a child assessment order this would provide the grounds for refusing the application.

15.26 Some parents, although willing to co-operate with the terms of a child assessment order, will have fears about the possible removal of their child as a result of the assessment. If used in the proper circumstances, follow-up provision to a child assessment order will normally be by way of services to the child and his family to remedy any harm identified. The professional practitioner will need to make this clear and to stress the importance of encouraging the child's development with Trust support where necessary. There will, however, be cases where the results of the assessment dictate that the child should live away from home. The professional practitioner must not shirk from his responsibility in discussing this possibility and emphasising the benefits that will flow from the parents working in partnership with the Trust in these circumstances. Parents whose children have a disability may be particularly worried by this kind of intervention and will require sensitive handling and reassurance that the intention is to enhance the life and abilities of their child, and that there is no intention to undermine their relationship with their child.

15.27 Although there may be occasions when the most obvious need is for a medical assessment, an assessment should always have a multi-disciplinary dimension. The difficulties and needs of the child must always be seen in the context of his social needs and the abilities and limitations of the child's parents, extended family and the local community to meet these needs. All professional practitioners engaged in working with the family should be encouraged to contribute to a multi-disciplinary assessment both to pool information and to make proposals for future action to support the family.

15.28 A child assessment order puts the professional practitioners on notice and gives them up to seven days to conduct their assessment. This timescale was fixed with the intention of causing the least possible disruption to the child but allowing sufficient time for an assessment to produce the information required by professional workers and parents to formulate together plans for future action. In order to ensure that this work can be achieved within the timescale and that a detailed assessment programme can be presented to the court for it to

be able to make the necessary directions, the professional team will need to plan in advance the matters to be covered during the assessment, the practical arrangements for doing this work, and the best way to involve parents and minimise trauma to the child. It has to be accepted that it may not always be possible within the seven days to do more than an initial assessment and obtain an indication of whether further work is necessary. Practitioners should consider ways of extending the assessment period on a voluntary basis if this becomes necessary. If the parents remain uncooperative and there is sufficient information to satisfy the grounds, an interim care or supervision order with conditions should be sought. Where only one parent consents, no order would be required since Article 5(6) empowers one parent to act alone. However, if one parent objects it would be necessary to obtain an order to avoid the possibility of private law proceedings under Article 8 to resolve the dispute between the parents.

15.29   Parents should always be told that a child assessment order may be applied for if they persist in refusing to co-operate, the reasons for making the application, the legal effect and detailed implications of the order, and the court procedure that would be followed. This information may be sufficient to persuade them that the Trust is genuinely concerned about the child and that the parents should co-operate with the proposed voluntary arrangements. This information should be confirmed in writing, backed up by easily understandable leaflets outlining a Trust's powers and duties and the rights and responsibilities of parents.

CHILDREN ORDER

CHAPTER 16: POLICE POWERS TO PROTECT CHILDREN

16.1 The police have important powers in protecting children under Part VI of the Children Order. Where a constable has reasonable cause to believe that a child would otherwise be likely to suffer significant harm, the constable may remove the child to suitable accommodation and keep him there. Alternatively, the constable may take such steps as are reasonable to ensure that the child's removal from hospital, or other place in which the child is being accommodated, is prevented (Article 65(1)). When a constable has exercised this power the child is referred to as having been taken into police protection (Article 65(2)). No child may be kept in police protection for more than 72 hours (Article 65(8)).

16.2 The power to take a child into police protection might be used to hold children such as runaways and glue-sniffers or whose parents had abandoned them. It may also be used where a constable attends a domestic dispute and finds a child living in conditions which constitute a threat to health and safety. A child can only be taken into police protection once the constable has found the child since there are no powers of search attached to Article 65. However, the police have existing powers to enter and search any premises without warrant if life or limb are endangered under Article 19(1)(e) of the Police and Criminal Evidence (Northern Ireland) Order 1989. Also, under Article 27(3)(e) of that Order the police may arrest without warrant any person who has committed any offence where the arrest is necessary to protect the child from that person.

16.3 As soon as is practicable after taking the child into police protection, the constable concerned has to ensure that the case is inquired into by a designated officer (Article 65(3)). Article 65(4) defines the term "designated officer" as meaning a police officer who is designated for the purposes of this Article by either the Chief Constable of the RUC or such other police officer as the Chief Constable may direct. That officer, on completing the inquiry, has to release the child from police protection unless he considers that there is still reasonable cause for believing that the child would be likely to suffer significant harm if released (Article 65(7)).

CHILDREN ORDER

Protection - responsibilities of designated officer

16.4   As soon as is reasonably practicable after a child has been taken into police protection, there are a number of responsibilities which the designated officer must undertake. These are to:

(a)   inform the Trust within whose area the child was found of the steps that have been, and are proposed to be taken, with respect to the child (under Article 65) and the reasons for taking them (Article 65(5)(a));

(b)   give details to the Trust within whose area the child is ordinarily resident of the place at which the child is being accommodated (Article 65(5)(b));

(c)   inform the child (if he seems capable of understanding) of the steps that have been taken, the reasons for taking them and of further steps that may be taken under this Article (Article 65(5)(c));

(d)   take such steps as are reasonably practicable to discover the wishes and feelings of the child (Article 65(5)(d));

(e)   where the child was taken into police protection other than to accommodation provided on behalf of a Trust or to a refuge, ensure that the child is moved to such accommodation (Article 65(5)(e));

(f)   take such steps as are reasonably practicable to give information to the child's parents, every other person who is not a parent but who has parental responsibility for the child and any other person with whom the child was living immediately before being taken into police protection. The information to be given is, again, the steps that the designated officer has taken under Article 65 with respect to the child, the reasons for taking them and the further steps that may be taken (Article 65(6)).

Parental responsibility

16.5   While a child is being kept in police protection, neither the constable concerned nor the designated officer acquire parental

responsibility. The designated officer must nevertheless do what is reasonable in all the circumstances to promote the child's welfare, bearing in mind the length of time police protection will last (Article 65(9) - see also Article 6(5)).

Contact with the child

16.6 The designated officer must also allow a range of persons to have contact with the child, as is, in the officer's opinion, both reasonable and in the child's best interests. These are the child's parents, anyone else who has parental responsibility for the child or with whom the child was living immediately before he was taken into police protection, any person who has in his favour an order relating to contact with the child or any person acting on behalf of any of the above. If the child in police protection is accommodated by the Trust for the area in which he usually lives, the Trust is required to afford such contact to these persons (Article 65(11)). As with all Articles of the Children Order relating to contact, the feelings and wishes of the child should be fully considered.

Inter-agency liaison

16.7 Trusts will find it necessary to monitor and review at regular intervals their channels of communication with the police so that effective inter-agency working is achieved. Trusts will need to build on existing practice and guidelines developed under the aegis of the Area Child Protection Committee and the principles set out in **Volume 6: Co-operating to Protect Children**. This should ensure that no child taken into police protection need be accommodated in a police station. It should also ensure that police action to safeguard a child is not prompted because of a belief that the evidence is not sufficient for an application for an emergency protection order.

CHILDREN ORDER

17.1   Anyone who knowingly and without lawful authority or reasonable excuse takes a child away from the person responsible for his care by virtue of a care order, an emergency protection order or police protection, commits an offence (Article 68(1)(a) and (2)). It is also an offence to keep a child away in these circumstances or induce, assist or incite the child to run away or stay away from the responsible person (Article 68(1)(b) and (c)). The term "responsible person" means any person who for the time being has care of the child by virtue of a care order, an emergency protection order or as a result of the police taking the child into police protection (Articles 68(2) and 69).

17.2   Where a voluntary children's home, a privately run children's home, or Trust or voluntary organisation foster parents provide a refuge for children who appear to be at risk of harm, and have been issued with a certificate by the Department of Health and Social Services under Article 70, the home or foster parent is exempt from the provisions of Article 68 (see Volume 4).

Recovery orders

17.3   A court may make a recovery order in respect of a child if there is reason to believe that the child has been unlawfully taken away or is being unlawfully kept away from the person responsible for him under a care order, or an emergency protection order or who is responsible for the exercise of police powers of protection; the child has run away or is staying away from that person; or the child is missing. Although the Trust should promptly notify the police of all children looked after who abscond or are abducted, so that inquiries to trace the child may be instigated, the court's powers to make a recovery order are restricted to those children who are in care, are the subject of an emergency protection order or are in police protection (Articles 68(2) and 69).

17.4   The recovery order can only be made on the application of any person who has parental responsibility for the child by virtue of a care order, an emergency protection order or, where the child is in police protection, the designated officer (Article 69(4)). The recovery order must name any person who has parental responsibility for the child by virtue of a care order or emergency protection order or, where the child is in police protection, the designated officer (Article 69(5)). It has also to name (or describe) the child. The application may be made **ex parte**.

17.5 A recovery order operates to secure the return of a missing child in the following way:

(a) it directs any person who is in a position to produce the child to do so, on request, to any authorised person;

(b) it authorises the child's removal by any authorised person;

(c) it requires any person who has information as to the child's whereabouts to disclose that information, on request, to a constable or officer of the court;

(d) it authorises a constable to enter specified premises and search for the child, using reasonable force if necessary (Article 69(3)). The premises may only be specified if it appears to the court that there are reasonable grounds for believing the child to be on them (Article 69(6)).

17.6 An "authorised person" in this context means any person specified by the court or a constable. It can also mean anyone specifically authorised for the purpose after the recovery order is made, by a person who has parental responsibility for the child by virtue of a care order or an emergency protection order. A Trust may therefore arrange for someone else to remove the child on its behalf once the order has been made. The power to search premises, however, can only be exercised by the police.

17.7 Where a person is authorised he must, if asked to do so (and should, in any event), produce some duly authenticated document showing that he is authorised and that this is related to the identified recovery order. Obstructing a person exercising his power to remove a child is an offence (Article 69(9) and (10)). When an authorised person requires a person to disclose information about the whereabouts of the child, that person cannot be excused from complying with the request on the grounds that it might incriminate him or his spouse of an offence (Article 69(11)).

17.8 Where a child is made the subject of a recovery order whilst being looked after by a Trust, any reasonable expenses incurred by an authorised person in giving effect to the order should be recoverable from the Trust (Article 69(12)).

CHAPTER 18: SECURE ACCOMMODATION ORDERS

18.1   Restricting the liberty of children is a serious step which must be taken only when there is no genuine alternative which would be appropriate. It must be a "last resort" in the sense that all else must first have been comprehensively considered and rejected. It must never be used because no other placement was available at the relevant time, because of inadequacies in staffing, because the child is simply being a nuisance or runs away and is not likely to suffer significant harm in doing so, and never as a form of punishment. It is important, in considering the possibility of a secure placement, that there is a clear view of the aims and objectives of such a placement and that those providing the accommodation can fully meet those aims and objectives.

18.2   Guidance in this chapter is confined to the basic requirements of Article 44 and the associated Secure Accommodation Regulations. Further guidance on the good practice and case management of a child in a secure unit is contained in **Volume 4: Residential Care**.

Criteria for the restriction of liberty

18.3   The use of secure accommodation by Trusts is subject to restrictions both in terms of the circumstances in which children they are looking after may be locked up and the maximum periods for which such accommodation may be used, with or without a court order. (See the Secure Accommodation Regulations at Annex C). Where such placements are to exceed 72 hours, the Trust must seek the authority of the court. Children in voluntary children's homes and privately run children's homes may not be kept in secure accommodation.

18.4   No child described above may be placed, or kept, in accommodation provided for the purpose of restricting liberty unless it appears that:

(a)   (i)   the child has a history of absconding and is likely to abscond from any other description of accommodation; and

      (ii)   if the child absconds, he is likely to suffer significant harm; or

(b)   if the child is kept in any other description of accommodation the child is likely to injure himself or other persons.

(Article 44(2): for meaning of "harm" and whether harm is "significant" see Articles 2(2) and 50(3) and the discussion in paragraphs 9.21 et seq).

18.5   A child meeting the above criteria may be placed in secure accommodation. It will be for the Trust itself to determine whether any criteria are met. The order of a court is not needed where the use of secure accommodation is for not more than 72 hours in aggregate in any period of 28 days.

Applications to the court

18.6   As it is not usually possible to predict accurately the need for secure accommodation, the short-term provisions outlined above will enable a Trust to deal with the situation when it arises. In this period consideration should be given to whether secure accommodation needs to be available as a longer-term option. If so, an application to the court will be required to keep the child in secure accommodation. Such applications may only be made by the Trust looking after the child (regulation 4 of the Secure Accommodation Regulations). Applications are generally made to the family proceedings court except that an application may be made to the county court or High Court where other proceedings specified in rules of court are pending in respect of the same child.

Role of the court

18.7   It is the role of the court to safeguard the child's welfare from inappropriate or unnecessary use of secure accommodation, by satisfying itself that those making the application have

demonstrated that the statutory criteria in Article 44(2) have been met (Article 44(4)). If the court determines that the criteria are satisfied, the court shall make an order authorising the child to be kept in secure accommodation and specifying the maximum period the child may be so kept (Article 44(5)). This, however, is subject to the power of the court to make an interim order under Article 44(6).

Guardians *ad litem*

18.8 Applications to keep a child in secure accommodation are "specified proceedings" within the meaning of Article 60 and rules of court. The court is required to appoint a guardian *ad litem* for the child unless it is satisfied that it is not necessary to do so in the interests of the child.

Legal representation

18.9 A court must not exercise the powers conferred by Article 44 unless the child who is the subject of the application is legally represented in that court. The guardian *ad litem* will appoint and instruct a solicitor for the child in accordance with the normal powers and duties prescribed by rules of court and the solicitor will represent the child as in other specified proceedings. The only exception is where a child, having been informed of his right to apply for legal aid and having had the opportunity to do so, has refused or failed to apply (Article 44(7)). The provision of legal aid in such proceedings is described in Article 172 of the Children Order which, by amendment to Article 5 of the Legal Aid, Advice and Assistance (Northern Ireland) Order 1981, requires that representation must be granted where a child who is brought before a court under Article 44 is not, but wished to be, legally represented before the court.

Interim orders

18.10 Where the court is not in a position to decide whether the criteria in Article 44(2) are met and adjourns consideration of the application, it may make an interim order permitting the child to be kept during the period of adjournment in secure accommodation (Article 44(6)).

Length of order

18.11 In determining the length of the order the court will have regard to the duty imposed on a Trust by Article 26(1) of the Children Order, to safeguard and promote the welfare of the child. Secure placements, once made, should only be for so long as is necessary and unavoidable.

18.12 The maximum periods a court may authorise a child to be kept in secure accommodation are:

(a) three months, on first application to the court (regulation 7 of the Secure Accommodation Regulations). This will include the period of a prior interim order, and the time limit runs from the making of the order; or

(b) six months, in respect of any further application to the court to continue to keep that child in secure accommodation (regulation 8 of the Secure Accommodation Regulations).

18.13 The order is permissive, ie a Trust is not required to use secure accommodation; it is authorised to use it when necessary and may only do so for as long as the statutory criteria are satisfied. A Trust looking after a child in secure accommodation in a home provided under Part VII of the Children Order must appoint at least three persons, at least one of whom is independent of the Trust, to review the keeping of the child in such accommodation within the first month and thereafter at intervals not exceeding three months (regulation 10 of the Secure Accommodation Regulations).

Appeals

18.14 The arrangements for appeals against the granting, or otherwise,

CHILDREN ORDER

of authority to keep a child in secure accommodation are set out in Article 166 of the Children Order. Both the child and the Trust making application to the family proceedings court may appeal to the county court against the making, or refusal to make, an order under Article 44.

CHILDREN ORDER

CHAPTER 19: TRANSITIONAL ARRANGEMENTS

19.1   This guidance seeks to expand on the contents and effect of Schedule 8 to the Children Order (Transitionals and Savings). The guidance is intended primarily as a checklist for action that may be required either before or after implementation and as an aid. Definitive interpretation of legal provisions can necessarily only be provided by the courts. The guidance focuses on public law orders and surrounding issues, commenting on private law concerns only where they appear relevant to Trusts.

Pending proceedings

19.2   These will cover nearly all cases where proceedings have been commenced, even though there has not yet been a court hearing. They will include wardship proceedings (subject to the comments below), and also cases where an appeal has been lodged, or time to appeal has not yet expired.

19.3   In all pending proceedings, the case will continue as if the Children Order did not exist, until a final order is made. The order made will thus be that provided for under the old law. Such an order will then be deemed to be an order in force immediately before the commencement of the Children Order and the appropriate transitional arrangements will apply (see below). This order will not, however, be backdated, but will have effect only from the date the final court order was made.

19.4   Depending on the date proceedings were instituted and the stage reached prior to commencement of the Children Order, Trusts will wish to consider whether to carry on with the existing proceedings or whether to withdraw their application and initiate new proceedings under the new jurisdiction.

19.5   Exceptions to the "pending" provision are proceedings under Article 45(3) of the Matrimonial Causes (Northern Ireland) Order 1978, section 12 of the Criminal Law Amendment Act 1885 and section 1(4) of the Punishment of Incest Act 1908. These will cease to have effect as parents always retain parental responsibility (Article 5(1)). For the same, reason an order already in existence under these enactments will, on commencement of the Children Order, cease to have effect.

CHILDREN ORDER

Trusts will need to consider whether there are any child protection issues at stake and take appropriate action.

Custody and care and control orders

19.6 Existing orders regarding custody, legal custody, care and control and access continue to have effect after the Children Order comes into operation. The fact that a person has parental responsibility for a child under the Children Order does not mean that he may act incompatibly with an existing order (paragraphs 5(3) and 6(3) of Schedule 8).

19.7 A person who otherwise would not have parental responsibility for the child but who had care and control or custody of a child under an existing order is given parental responsibility while that order lasts. Thus, a father who does not have parental responsibility for his child because he is not married to the child's mother, but who had care and control or custody under an existing order, is deemed to have a parental responsibility order in his favour (paragraph 5(4) of Schedule 8). Any other person who had care and control or custody by virtue of an existing order, and who is not a parent or guardian of the child, is given parental responsibility for the duration of the existing order (paragraph 6(1) of Schedule 8). Such a person is also treated in specific instances as if he had the benefit of a residence order (he may apply for an Article 8 order without leave - paragraph 6(3) of Schedule 8). A person with an access order under the old law is not given parental responsibility but may apply for a contact order (paragraph 8 of Schedule 8).

19.8 Existing orders regarding custody, legal custody, care and control and access may be discharged by a court, either on application or of its own motion in family proceedings (paragraph 10(3) of Schedule 8). They may also be brought to an end if the court makes a residence order or care order under the Children Order (paragraph 10(1) of Schedule 8).

Children in care

19.9 All children in the care of the Department of Health and Social Services or a Trust by virtue of -

(a)   a parental rights order under section 104 of the Children and Young Persons Act (Northern Ireland) 1968;

(b)   a fit person order made under section 66, 74, 95, 96, 97, 143 or 144 of the Children and Young Persons Act (Northern Ireland) 1968;

(c)   an order which by virtue of regulations made under section 101 of the Children Act 1989 has effect as if it were an order made under section 95(1)(b) of the Children and Young Persons Act (Northern Ireland) 1968;

(d)   an order under section 74 of the Social Work (Scotland) Act 1968 or section 25 of the Children and Young Persons Act 1969 in respect of a child who moves from England, Scotland or Wales to Northern Ireland;

(e)   an order made in matrimonial proceedings under Article 46 of the Matrimonial Causes (Northern Ireland) Order 1978; an order made in domestic proceedings under Article 12 of the Domestic Proceedings (Northern Ireland) Order 1980; an order made on refusal of an adoption order under Article 27(1)(b) of the Adoption (Northern Ireland) Order 1987; or

(e)   a final order made in exercise of the High Court's inherent jurisdiction;

are deemed to be in the care of the same body under Article 50 of the Children Order (paragraph 11 of Schedule 8).

19.10   All children under the care of the manager of a training school by virtue of a training school order made under section 95, 108(a) or 143(6)(b) of the Children and Young Persons Act (Northern Ireland) 1968 are deemed to be in the care of the Trust in whose area they are ordinarily resident under Article 50 of the Children Order (paragraph 30 of Schedule 8).

19.11   Interim orders made in exercise of the High Court's inherent jurisdiction committing a child to the care of the Department of Health and Social Services or a Trust are deemed to be pending proceedings for a maximum period of twelve months from commencement of the Children Order (paragraph 1(2) of

Schedule 8) during which time the wardship continues (regardless of the provisions of paragraph 13 of Schedule 8). Such proceedings should be brought back to court at the earliest opportunity (consistent with the best interests of the child) and if a final order is made in the exercise of the High Court's inherent jurisdiction, this will be deemed to be a care order under Article 50 of the Children Order and the wardship will cease. The proceedings will not be treated as pending at the end of twelve months if no final order has been made by that date. At that point any outstanding orders will convert to care orders under Article 50 of the Children Order and the wardship will cease from that date.

19.12 In the light of these transitional arrangements, Trusts will need to amend their records to ensure the child's correct legal status is noted and consider whether or not to apply to discharge or vary the order where the circumstances of the case, and the welfare of the child, suggest that this, and particularly lesser intervention, would be appropriate.

19.13 The implications of these provisions where a care order is deemed to be made, include:

Contact

(i) The provisions of the Children Order will apply. This means, for example, there will be a presumption that contact will be allowed with parents (see Article 53). Contact cannot generally be refused without a court order except in an emergency for a maximum of seven days.

Consultation

(ii) Not only a child in care has the right to be consulted about any decision relating to him, so far as practicable (Article 26(2)), but so also do his parents, non-parents with parental responsibility and anyone else the Trust considers relevant. The Trust must also consider the child's religious persuasion, racial origin and cultural and linguistic background (Article 26(3)).

Secure Accommodation

(iii)   The secure accommodation provisions will apply (Article 44).

Review Regulations

(iv)   The child's care must be reviewed at intervals specified in the Review of Children's Cases Regulations.

Complaints Procedure

(v)   The child, his parents, Trust foster parents (and others specified in Article 45(3)) will have access to a new complaints procedure with an independent element, and the opportunity to appear before a panel, also including an independent person.

Advise, Assist and Befriend

(vi)   Young persons who cease to be looked after by a Trust after reaching their 16th birthday will qualify for advice and assistance until their 21st birthday. Aftercare provision will need to be developed for young people due to leave care or accommodation, and for those who may already have left when aged 16 or over and have yet to reach their 21st birthday.

Directions and injunctions

19.14   Although an order falling within paragraph 11(3)(d) or (e) of Schedule 8 will be deemed to be a care order under Article 50 of the Children Order, if the court gave directions when making the order (whether by Article 46(5)(a) of the Matrimonial Causes (Northern Ireland) Order 1978 or by virtue of the High Court's inherent jurisdiction) those directions shall continue to have effect until varied or discharged by the court that made them (paragraph 12(4) of Schedule 8). This is so despite any provision in the

Children Order to the contrary, except that it is subject to the secure accommodation provisions in Article 44 and regulations made under that Article (paragraph 12(5) of Schedule 8). In particular, where directions have authorised restricting the child's liberty, those directions shall expire at the end of three months from the commencement of the Children Order, although a court could extend them for further periods of six months in accordance with the Secure Accommodation Regulations.

19.15　As soon after commencement of the Children Order as is reasonably practicable, Trusts should consider, as part of their assessment of all orders made in their favour, whether to seek a discharge or variation of these directions. This will be particularly relevant where the directions may no longer be appropriate or in the child's interests.

19.16　Where a Trust initiated wardship proceedings prior to the commencement of the Children Order solely for the purpose of obtaining an injunction, the injunction will remain live until varied or discharged. Similarly, any injunction granted where a child is a ward of court and in care by virtue of a final order under a specified statute, or in the exercise of the High Court's inherent jurisdiction, will remain in force until varied or discharged, even though the order is deemed a care order under the Children Order and the wardship ceases. Action for breach of the injunction will be heard in the High Court that made the order.

Wardship

19.17　Where a child is a ward of court and, in proceedings that are not pending, is in the care of the Department of Health and Social Services or a Trust in the exercise of the High Court's inherent jurisdiction, the wardship will cease on commencement of Part V of the Children Order (paragraph 13(1) of Schedule 8). The child will be deemed to be in care under a care order made under Article 50 of the Children Order (paragraph 11 of Schedule 8). Any directions which the wardship made will continue, subject to the general rules about directions.

19.18　Where a child has been placed or allowed to remain in the care

of the Department or a Trust in wardship under an interim order, the wardship proceedings will no longer be treated as pending one year after the commencement of paragraph 1(2) of Schedule 8 to the Children Order if no final order has been made by that date. At that point (or earlier, if a final committal to care is ordered), the child will become subject to a deemed care order under Article 50 of the Children Order and the wardship will cease.

19.19 Similarly, if a child is in the care of the Department or a Trust under the Children and Young Persons Act (Northern Ireland) 1968 and is then made a ward of court **before** the commencement of Part V of the Children Order, and thereafter remains in care, the wardship will cease on the commencement of Part V. The child will become subject to a deemed care order under Article 50 of the Children Order (paragraph 13(2) of Schedule 8).

19.20 If the child is a ward of court but not in care on the commencement date of the Children Order, and a care order under Article 50 is subsequently made, the wardship ceases when the care order is made (Article 179(4)).

Contributions towards the maintenance of children looked after by Trusts

19.21 Paragraph 19 of Schedule 8 refers to various statutory provisions by which either parent may be required to pay maintenance for a child in care. Under the transitional arrangements an order made under these statutory provisions will be converted to a contribution order made under Article 41 of the Children Order.

Supervision orders made under the Children and Young Persons Act (Northern Ireland) 1968

19.22 Any supervision order made under the Children and Young Persons Act (Northern Ireland) 1968 placing a child under the supervision of the Department of Health and Social Services or a Trust will be deemed to be a supervision order made under Article 50 of the Children Order. Similarly, a supervision order made under the 1968 Act placing a child under the supervision of an education and library board will be deemed to be an

education supervision order made under Article 55 of the Children Order. If there is a requirement for the child to reside with a named person, this will remain for as long as the order is in force, unless the court directs otherwise. Any other requirements of the court, or directions given by the supervisor, will be deemed to have been made under Schedule 3 or 4 to the Children Order.

19.23   A supervision order or an education supervision order under the Children Order normally lasts for up to twelve months. Transitionally, if the order had been in force on commencement of Part V of the Children Order for six months or more, it will cease to have effect at the end of six months beginning with the commencement of Part V of the Children Order. Exceptions are where it ceases to have effect earlier because a care order is made (see Article 179(3)), or it would have expired earlier were it not for the Children Order, or the court directs otherwise (but this must not exceed three years and it is intended that the three-year period runs from the date the order was first made). If the order had been in force for less than six months, it will run for one year from the commencement of Part V of the Children Order, subject to the same provisions as above. The Trust (or education and library board) will wish to consider what, if any, further alternative action is required. If an extension is sought, the application will have to be made to the court **after** the date of commencement of the Children Order but **before** the date on which the order would otherwise have expired. Where the Trust wishes to obtain a care order in place of the supervision order it must first satisfy the court of the criteria in Article 50.

Other supervision orders

19.24   Supervision orders under Article 47 of the Matrimonial Causes (Northern Ireland) Order 1978, Article 11 of the Domestic Proceedings (Northern Ireland) Order 1980 and Article 27(1)(a) of the Adoption (Northern Ireland) Order 1987 are not deemed to be supervision orders under Article 50. Such orders will continue in force for one year from the commencement of the Children Order unless the order would have ceased to have effect earlier, or the court directs that it should end earlier. Again, the Trust will wish to consider what further action should be taken.

CHILDREN ORDER

Place of safety orders

19.25 A place of safety order or warrant made under any of the provisions listed in paragraph 23(2) of Schedule 8 shall continue to have effect as if the Children Order had not been brought into operation. In addition, any statutory provision repealed by the Children Order shall continue to have effect so far as is necessary for carrying out the place of safety order, as if the Children Order were not in operation.

19.26 The effect of this is that warrants or orders authorising the removal of a child to a place of safety under the Children and Young Persons Act (Northern Ireland) 1968 or Article 35 of the Adoption (Northern Ireland) Order 1987 will continue unaffected by the Children Order. Interim orders made under section 101 of the 1968 Act will continue to have effect as if the Children Order had not been made, but no further interim orders can be made under the old legislation.

Training school orders

19.27 On the commencement of Part V of the Children Order, a child subject to a training school order made under section 95, 108(a) or 143(6)(b) of the Children and Young Persons Act (Northern Ireland) 1968 will be treated as a child subject to a care order made under Article 50 of the Children Order (paragraph 30 of Schedule 8). It will be necessary for the managers of training schools to identify those children in their care who are subject to such orders and notify the Trust in whose area the child is ordinarily resident. It will then be necessary for the Trust to make suitable arrangements to take over the care of the child. If the person is over the age of 18 when Part V of the Children Order comes into operation, the training school order will cease to have effect from that date.

19.28 Each deemed care order should be reviewed by the appropriate Trust (ie the Trust in whose area the child is ordinarily resident) within six months of the commencement of Part V of the Children Order. The review will follow the general review procedure for children in care (Article 45) which will require each reviewing Trust to consider what action to take under the Children Order, including considering whether to apply to the

court for the discharge of the deemed care order and notifying the results of the review to the child, his parents and others with parental responsibility for the child and other relevant persons.

19.29   Training school orders deemed to be care orders will expire when the child reaches age 18. This expiry date may, on occasions, be before the date on which the training school order would have expired if Part V of the Children Order had not been brought into operation, but its discharge will be consistent with other care orders made under Article 50 of the Children Order. Conversely, the deemed care order shall not extend beyond the date the training school order would ordinarily have ceased.

MAIN COURT STRUCTURE

COURT OF APPEAL

●   Appeals from High Court and divorce county courts

HIGH COURT

●   Appeals from a family care centre

●   Exceptionally grave, important or complex cases transferred from family care centre

●   Private law applications arising in the course of other proceedings

●   Inherent jurisdiction

DIVORCE COUNTY COURT

●   Private law applications which arise in the course of other proceedings

COUNTY COURT

●   Appeals from a domestic proceedings court

FAMILY CARE CENTRE

●   Appeals from a family proceedings court

●   Exceptionally grave, important or complex cases transferred from family proceedings court

DOMESTIC PROCEEDINGS COURT

●   Private law applications which arise in the course of other proceedings

FAMILY PROCEEDINGS COURT

●   Most public law applications

●   Free-standing private law applications

THRESHOLD CRITERIA FOR CARE AND SUPERVISION ORDERS

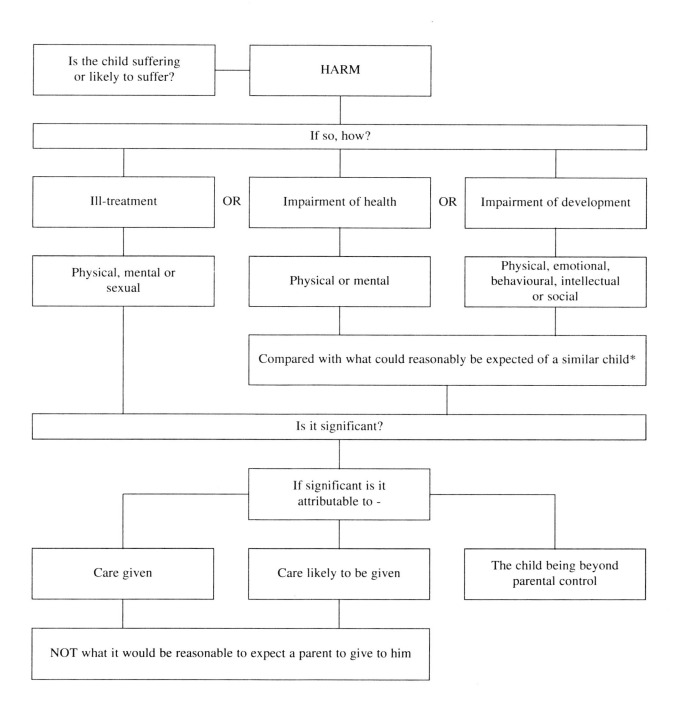

*Note: see Article 50 (3)

STATUTORY RULES OF NORTHERN IRELAND

1996   No. 487

CHILDREN

The Children (Secure Accommodation) Regulations (Northern Ireland) 1996

Made ....   *10th October 1996*

Coming into operation ....   *4th November 1996*

ARRANGEMENT OF REGULATIONS

The Department of Health and Social Services, in exercise of the powers conferred on it by Articles 44(3) and (8), 45(1) and (2), 73(1) and (2)(d), 89(1), (2)(f) and (3), 105(1), (2)(f) and (3) of the Children (Northern Ireland) Order 1995(**a**) and of all other powers enabling it in that behalf, hereby makes the following Regulations:

(**a**)   S.I. 1995/755 (N.I. 2)

Citation, commencement and interpretation

1.—(1) These Regulations may be cited as the Children (Secure Accommodation) Regulations (Northern Ireland) 1996 and shall come into operation on 4th November 1996.

(2) In these Regulations -

"the Order" means the Children (Northern Ireland) Order 1995;

"authority home" means a home provided by an authority under Part VII of the Order;

"independent visitor" means a person appointed under Article 31(1);

"secure accommodation" means accommodation which is provided for the purpose of restricting the liberty of children to whom Article 44 applies.

(3) Any notice required under these Regulations is to be given in writing and may be sent by ordinary post.

(4) In these Regulations, any reference to a numbered Article is to the Article of the Order bearing that number.

Placement of a child aged under 13 in secure accommodation

2. Article 44 shall be modified in relation to a child under the age of 13 years of age so that a child under the age of 13 years shall not be placed in secure accommodation in an authority home without the prior approval of the Department.

Children to whom Article 44 shall not apply

3.ƒ(1) Article 44 shall not apply to a child who is detained under any provision of the Mental Health (Northern Ireland) Order 1986(**a**).

(2) Article 44 shall not apply to a child —

(a) to whom Article 21(5) (accommodation of persons over 16 but under 21) applies and who is being accommodated under that Article; or

(b) in respect of whom an order has been made under Article 62 (child assessment order) and who is kept away from home pursuant to that order.

(**a**) S.I. 1986/595 (N.I. 4)

Applications to court

4. Applications to a court under Article 44 in respect of a child who is being looked after by an authority shall be made only by that authority.

Duty to give notice of placement in an authority home

5. Where a child is placed in secure accommodation in an authority home which is managed by an authority other than the authority which is looking after him, the authority which manages that accommodation shall give notice to the authority which is looking after him that he has been placed there, within 12 hours of his being placed there.

Maximum period in secure accommodation without court authority

6.—(1) Subject to paragraph (2), the maximum period beyond which a child to whom Article 44 applies may not be kept in secure accommodation without the authority of a court is an aggregate of 72 hours (whether or not consecutive) in any period of 28 consecutive days.

(2) Where authority of a court to keep a child in secure accommodation has been given, any period during which the child has been kept in such accommodation before the giving of that authority shall be disregarded for the purposes of calculating the maximum period in relation to any subsequent occasion on which the child is placed in such accommodation after the period authorised by the court has expired.

Maximum initial period of authorisation by a court

7. Subject to regulation 8, the maximum period for which a court may authorise a child to whom Article 44 applies to be kept in secure accommodation is 3 months.

Further periods of authorisation by a court

8. A court may authorise a child to whom Article 44 applies to be kept in secure accommodation for a further period not exceeding 6 months at any one time.

Duty to notify parents and others in relation to children in secure accommodation in an authority home

9. Where a child to whom Article 44 applies is kept in secure accommodation in an authority home and it is intended that an application will be made to a court to keep the child in that accommodation, the authority which is looking after the child shall, if practicable, give notice of that intention, as soon as possible, to —

(a) his parents;

(b) any person who is not a parent of his but who has parental responsibility for him;

(c) the child's independent visitor, if one has been appointed; and

(d) any other person who that authority considers should be informed.

Appointment of persons to review placement in secure accommodation in an authority home

10.—(1) Subject to paragraph (2), each authority looking after a child in secure accommodation in an authority home shall appoint at least 3 persons who shall review the keeping of the child in such accommodation for the purposes of securing his welfare within one month of the inception of the placement and then at intervals not exceeding 3 months where the child continues to be kept in such accommodation.

(2) At least one of the persons appointed in accordance with paragraph (1) should not be a member, director or officer of the authority by or on behalf of which the child is being looked after.

Review of placement in secure accommodation in an authority home

11.—(1) The persons appointed under regulation 10 to review the keeping of a child in secure accommodation shall have regard to whether or not —

(a) the criteria for keeping the child in secure accommodation continue to apply;

(b) the placement in such accommodation in an authority home continues to be necessary; and

(c) any other description of accommodation would be appropriate for him,

and in doing so shall have regard to the welfare of the child whose case is being reviewed.

(2) Before conducting the review referred to in regulation 10, the persons appointed shall, unless it is not reasonably practicable to do so, seek the views of —

(a) the child;

(b) any parent of his;

(c) any person not being a parent of his but who has parental responsibility for him;

(d) any other person who has had the care of the child, whose views the persons appointed consider should be taken into account;

(e)   the child's independent visitor, if one has been appointed; and

(f)   the authority managing the secure accommodation in which the child is placed, if that authority is not the authority which is looking after the child.

(3) The authority shall, so far as is reasonably practicable, notify all those whose views have been sought under paragraph (2), of the details of the result of the review and what action, if any, the authority proposes to take in relation to the child in the light of the review, and its reasons for taking or not taking such action.

Records to be kept in respect of a child in secure accommodation in an authority home

12. Whenever a child is placed in secure accommodation in an authority home, the authority which manages that accommodation shall ensure that a record is kept of —

(a)   the name, date of birth and sex of that child;

(b)   the care order or other statutory provision by virtue of which the child is in the home and in either case particulars of any other authority involved with the placement of the child in that home;

(c)   the date and time of his placement in secure accommodation, the reason for his placement, the name of the officer authorising the placement and where the child was living before the placement;

(d)   all those notified by virtue of regulation 9 or 11(3) in their application to the child;

(e)   court orders made in respect of the child by virtue of Article 44;

(f)   reviews undertaken in respect of the child by virtue of regulation 10;

(g)   the date and time of any occasion on which the child is locked on his own in any room in the secure accommodation other than his bedroom during usual bedtime hours, the name of the person authorising this action, the reason for it and the date on which and time at which the child ceases to be locked in that room; and

(h)   the date and time of his discharge and his address following discharge from secure accommodation,

and the Department may require copies of these records to be sent to it at any time.

Voluntary homes and registered children's homes not to be used for restricting liberty

13.—(1) The use of accommodation for the purpose of restricting the liberty of children in voluntary homes and registered children's homes is prohibited.

(2) The contravention of, or failure to comply with, the provisions of paragraph (1), without reasonable excuse, shall be an offence against these Regulations(**a**).

Sealed with the Official Seal of the Department of Health and Social
Services on 10th October 1996.

(L.S.)

P. A. Conliffe
Assistant Secretary

(**a**)   A person who is guilty of an offence against these Regulations is liable to a fine not exceeding level 4 on the standard scale; *see* Articles 89(4) and 105(4) of the Children (Northern Ireland) Order 1995

EXPLANATORY NOTE

(This note is not part of the Regulations.)

These Regulations supplement the provisions in Article 44 of the Children (Northern Ireland) Order 1995 ("the Order") which govern the restriction of liberty of children who are being looked after by authorities.

The Regulations provide for approval by the Department of Health and Social Services to the placement of a child aged under 13 in secure accommodation (regulation 2); the children to whom Article 44 of the Order shall not apply (regulation 3); the making of applications to court (regulation 4); the duty to give notification of placements in authority homes (regulation 5); provision as to the maximum period in accommodation for restricting liberty without court authority (regulation 6); the maximum initial period of authorisation by any court (regulation 7); further periods of authorisation by a court (regulation 8); the duty to notify parents and others in relation to children in secure accommodation (regulation 9); the appointment of persons to review placements in secure accommodation (regulation 10); the review of placements in secure accommodation (regulation 11); the records to be kept in respect of a child in secure accommodation (regulation 12); and the prohibition of the use of accommodation for restricting liberty in voluntary homes and registered children's homes and breach thereof (regulation 13).

Articles 44(3) and (8), 45(1) and (2), 73(1) and (2)(d), 89(1), (2)(f) and (3), and 105(1), (2)(f) and (3) of the Order are the enabling provisions under which these Regulations are made. They were brought into operation on 18th July 1996 by virtue of Article 2(1) of, and Schedule 1 to, the Children (1995 Order) (Commencement No. 3) Order (Northern Ireland) 1996 (S.R. 1996 No. 297 (C.17)).

STATUTORY RULES OF NORTHERN IRELAND

1996   No. 435

CHILDREN

The Emergency Protection Order (Transfer of Responsibilities) Regulations (Northern Ireland) 1996

Made ....   *18th September 1996*

Coming into operation ....   *4th November 1996*

The Department of Health and Social Services, in exercise of the powers conferred on it by Article 71(3) and (4) of the Children (Northern Ireland) Order 1995 (**a**) and of all other powers enabling it in that behalf, hereby makes the following Regulations:

Citation and commencement

1.   These Regulations may be cited as the Emergency Protection Order (Transfer of Responsibilities) Regulations (Northern Ireland) 1996 and shall come into operation on 4th November 1996.

Transfer of responsibilities under emergency protection orders

2. Subject to regulation 5, where —

(a)   an emergency protection order has been made with respect to a child;

(b)   the applicant for the order was not the authority within whose area the child is ordinarily resident; and

(c)   that authority is of the opinion that it would be in the child's best interests for the applicant's responsibilities under the order to be transferred to it,

that authority shall (subject to its having complied with the requirements imposed by regulation 3(1)) be treated, for the purposes of the Children (Northern Ireland) Order 1995, as though it and not the original applicant had applied for, and been granted, the order.

(**a**)   S.I. 1995/755 (N.I.2)

Requirements to be complied with by authorities

3.—(1) In forming its opinion under regulation 2(c) the authority shall consult the applicant for the emergency protection order and have regard to the following considerations —

    (a)   the ascertainable wishes and feelings of the child having regard to his age and understanding;

    (b)   the child's physical, emotional and educational needs for the duration of the emergency protection order;

    (c)   the likely effect on him of any change in his circumstances which may be caused by a transfer of responsibilities under the order;

    (d)   his age, sex and family background;

    (e)   the circumstances which gave rise to the application for the emergency protection order;

    (f)   any directions of a court and other orders made in respect of the child;

    (g)   the relationship (if any) of the applicant for the emergency protection order to the child; and

    (h)   any plans which the applicant may have in respect of the child.

(2) The authority shall give notice, as soon as possible after it forms the opinion referred to in regulation 2(c), of the date and time of the transfer to —

    (a)   the court which made the emergency protection order;

    (b)   the applicant for the order; and

    (c)   those (other than the authority) to whom the applicant for the order gave notice of it.

(3) A notice required under this regulation shall be given in writing and may be sent by ordinary post.

When responsibility under emergency protection order transfers

4. The time at which responsibility under any emergency protection order is to be treated as having been transferred to an authority shall be the time stated as the time of transfer in the notice given in accordance with regulation 3 by the authority to the applicant for the emergency protection order or the time at which notice is given to him under that regulation, whichever is the later.

Exception for children in refuges

5. These Regulations shall not apply where the child to whom the emergency protection order applies is in a refuge in respect of which there is in force a certificate issued by the Department under Article 70 of the Children (Northern Ireland) Order 1995 (refuges for children at risk) and the person carrying on the home, or the foster parent providing the refuge, having taken account of the wishes and feelings of the child, has decided that the child should continue to be provided with the refuge for the duration of the order.

Sealed with the Official Seal of the Department of Health and Social
Services on 18th September 1996.

(L.S.)

P. A. Conliffe
Assistant Secretary

EXPLANATORY NOTE

(This note is not part of the Regulations.)

These Regulations make provision for an authority to be treated as though it and not the original applicant for an emergency protection order had applied for and been granted the order. They make provision for requirements to have been complied with before responsibility under the order is transferred and for the time the transfer is to be treated as effected. The Regulations do not apply when the child who is the subject of the emergency protection order is in a refuge and the child is to continue to live there for the duration of the order.

Article 71(3) and (4) of the Children (Northern Ireland) Order 1995 is the enabling provision under which these Regulations are made. It was brought into operation on 18th July 1996 by virtue of Article 2(1) of, and Schedule 1 to, the Children (1995 Order) (Commencement No. 3) Order (Northern Ireland) 1996 (S.R. 1996 No.297 (C.17)).